Cambridge Elements ≡

Elements in Reinventing Capitalism
edited by
Arie Y. Lewin
Duke University
Till Talaulicar
University of Erfurt

TRANSFORMING OUR CRITICAL SYSTEMS

How Can We Achieve the Systemic Change the World Needs?

Geert-Jan van der Zanden
Sasin School of Management

Rozanne Henzen
Sasin School of Management

Shaftesbury Road, Cambridge CB2 8EA, United Kingdom

One Liberty Plaza, 20th Floor, New York, NY 10006, USA

477 Williamstown Road, Port Melbourne, VIC 3207, Australia

314–321, 3rd Floor, Plot 3, Splendor Forum, Jasola District Centre, New Delhi – 110025, India

103 Penang Road, #05–06/07, Visioncrest Commercial, Singapore 238467

Cambridge University Press is part of Cambridge University Press & Assessment, a department of the University of Cambridge.

We share the University's mission to contribute to society through the pursuit of education, learning and research at the highest international levels of excellence.

www.cambridge.org
Information on this title: www.cambridge.org/9781009475655

DOI: 10.1017/9781009410311

First published 2024

A catalogue record for this publication is available from the British Library.

ISBN 978-1-009-47565-5 Hardback
ISBN 978-1-009-41032-8 Paperback
ISSN 2634-8950 (online)
ISSN 2634-8942 (print)

Cambridge University Press & Assessment has no responsibility for the persistence or accuracy of URLs for external or third-party internet websites referred to in this publication and does not guarantee that any content on such websites is, or will remain, accurate or appropriate.

Transforming Our Critical Systems

How Can We Achieve the Systemic Change the World Needs?

Elements in Reinventing Capitalism

DOI: 10.1017/9781009410311
First published online: January 2024

Geert-Jan van der Zanden
Sasin School of Management

Rozanne Henzen
Sasin School of Management

Author for correspondence: Geert-Jan van der Zanden, gj.vanderzanden@sasin.edu

Abstract: Economic growth has catalysed enormous progress in the world, but we have entered an era of perverse economic growth, at the expense of social and natural capital. As the world runs further behind on the Sustainable Development Goals, managing and mitigating the looming environmental and social crises in an increasingly volatile, uncertain, complex and ambiguous world will be one of the biggest challenges, but also one of the biggest commercial opportunities, of our time. Building on earlier research on systemic change, using the WHAT-HOW-WHY framework, this Element presents actionable insights for the radical systemic reinvention of our 'critical systems' that satisfy human and societal needs such as nutrition, mobility, infrastructure and health. We highlight ten emerging paradigms for future-fit systemic change, discuss how stakeholder mindsets can be developed and present new skills for leaders and a pathway to enable companies to become drivers of collaborative transformation. This title is also available as Open Access on Cambridge Core.

This Element also has a video abstract:
www.cambridge.org/vanderzanden-henzen

Keywords: transformation, leadership, sustainability, systemic/system change, mindset, collaboration

ISBNs: 9781009475655 (HB), 9781009410328 (PB), 9781009410311 (OC)
ISSNs: 2634-8950 (online), 2634-8942 (print)

Contents

Prologue: The Purpose of This Element

Since the beginning of time, humanity has organised itself to satisfy its needs, from the basic needs of feeding, housing and staying safe and healthy to more elevated needs of developing and managing communities. As a result, we create tremendous wealth, live longer, get smarter, suffer less, enjoy richer experiences and our species has grown exponentially. We are left to wonder, though, is this the right measure of success?

To a large extent, mankind's success has come from its ability to harness nature. In the Netherlands, where we both grew up, a populous country, a third of which is below sea level, harnessing nature is part of the national psyche. But, unfortunately, our eagerness to harness nature has turned into a destructive force, eroding the very thing we are part of and depend on: nature.

Dutch culture is also very pragmatic and inquisitive, which has helped us question things, open our minds and learn while working and living in different countries around the world. This is where, for both of us, our curiosity originated to question and rethink the way mankind organises itself to satisfy its needs.

As societal imbalances and tensions between humanity and nature continue to escalate, mere incremental adjustments to legacy models are no longer sufficient. Instead, there is an urgent need for a radical, holistic and systemic transformation of our current models. Various scholars have acknowledged the immense challenges involved in deliberately altering complex systems, and we will delve into these complexities. The primary objective of this Element is to expand upon existing ideas and establish a connection between theoretical literature and practical approaches to accomplish actionable insights for systemic change. Moreover, the Element aims to explore the facilitation of necessary shifts in mindsets and cross-sector collaborations, with a specific focus on the business sector (and business education), whose crucial role in systemic change processes currently remains relatively under-explored.

In addition, from Geert-Jan: While escaping from the big city bustle, during reflexive hikes in Taiwan's mountainous cedar forests and dives in Southeast Asia's coral reefs, it became increasingly clear to me that our real measure of success should be to live in harmony with our natural and human environment, working with nature, not against it, and making sure we leave no one behind when we pursue wealth and well-being. This will be the biggest challenge and the biggest opportunity of our time.

Combining business studies in Europe and the USA and studies in environmental management and policy in Scandinavia with decades in business as a practitioner and executive adviser in sustainability transition, I am now honoured to be able to share my insights as a visiting professor at Sasin

School of Management, in Bangkok, helping to progress a sustainability mindset in a region that will be a pivotal hotspot in humanity's efforts to mitigate and adapt to the effects of climate change and resource depletion. Following an article on systemic change in *AACSB* magazine (Association to Advance Collegiate Schools of Business), Professor Arie Lewin requested me to share more on this topic in an Element in the Reinventing Capitalism series of Cambridge University Press. Given the very challenging trajectory the relationship between man and nature has been on this last century and the urgency for us to more radically and holistically address many of our complex societal problems, I am grateful for this opportunity and hope the frameworks and thoughts expressed in this Element will trigger further constructive thinking and action.

In addition, from Rozanne: I have been working within the fascinating world of sustainability and circularity for the last decade, first as a student, then as a researcher and author. It has become apparent that ideas on tackling our twenty-first-century challenges have been voiced by many, but the action needed is running behind. Humans are unique in the sense that we have the power to combine ideas, have thoughts about those ideas, share them with others, build on them and bring them to life. I want to call on you, our readers, to change your perspective from consumer to concerned citizen, and shift from individualistic thinking to we-thinking, to help magnify the power of these ideas. Not that the responsibility to solve our 21st-century problems lies with the individual; to me, it should be a combined multi-stakeholder effort, but all individuals have the ability to take that citizen perspective with them in their work and daily lives. And now, specifically to my fellow Millennials and Gen Z readers because we feel the weight of the world pressing down on us: we have the opportunity to create a new system in which we will not make the same mistakes our parents' and grandparents' generations did. With the help of creativity, innovation and trust in our capabilities, we can magnify our power to rethink, redesign and rearrange our future and our now.

Executive Summary

Economic growth has catalysed enormous progress in the world. However, focus on economic growth alone in many ways has become a destructive force, promoting short-term wins over long-term prosperity, depleting natural resources and widening exclusion. At the expense of social and natural capital, we have entered an increasingly perverse economic growth era. Environmental and social challenges constitute the most significant risks to businesses and society today. There is increasing awareness among leaders, consumers and capital providers that we must radically reinvent how we satisfy human and societal needs to manage and mitigate these risks. We need to reinvent the growth model for the societal and environmental realities of the twenty-first century, to work with nature, not against it, and create value in the long rather than the short term, for many, not just a privileged few.

Despite big governmental and corporate commitments towards the Sustainable Development Goals (SDGs), the world is running behind in the sustainability transition. To limit global warming to 1.5°C and avoid the chance of catastrophic impacts, CO_2-eq (CO_2 equivalent) emissions need to be reduced by 45 per cent from 2010 levels by 2030. Instead, based on all national commitments made as of March 2023, CO_2-eq emissions are expected to rise by 10 per cent by 2030. Moreover, as we get further behind in the implementation of these plans, the urgency and the need increase for radical system-level reinvention instead of marginal innovation of the 'critical systems' that satisfy our basic human needs, such as nutrition, mobility, infrastructure or health, and the 'supporting systems' that enable the critical ones, such as finance, energy, education or governance.

The need to achieve radical impact in a relatively short period is one of the biggest challenges and biggest commercial opportunities of our time. As a result, unprecedented governmental and private funding is becoming available for our systems' environmentally responsible and socially just reinvention.

Systems are complex because they involve multiple actors and stakeholders with often diverse objectives and priorities and numerous connected subsystems with governance contexts and dynamics of their own. Systems thinking gives us a valuable way to understand the relationships between the components and actors in a system and foresee the intended and the unintended ripple effects of our interventions in that system.

History has taught us that leverage points for systemic change are often counter-intuitive. In this Element, we expand upon existing ideas and establish a connection between theoretical literature and practical approaches to accomplish actionable insights for systemic change. We do this by analysing examples of systemic change efforts in multiple systems and geographies through the lens of a modification of the Systemic Intervention Framework originally introduced by Donella Meadows (1999). We categorise these intervention areas as WHY, HOW or WHAT, and bring forward the following practical insights:

1. WHAT without WHY interventions are likely to deliver suboptimal outcomes.
2. Lack of alignment between subsystems hinders systemic change.
3. Silver-bullet solutions require increased precaution to prevent unintended consequences.
4. WHY interventions require investment in collaborative processes.
5. Old mindsets are unlikely to produce a new system.
6. Big commitments need reinforcement.

Change is complex, and systemic change in today's volatile, uncertain, complex and ambiguous (VUCA) environment even more so. Practice shows that interventions dictated by one actor often realise limited or counterproductive impact at the system level because they lack a system understanding, a shared mindset and a shared vision across stakeholders. The successful reinvention of systems therefore requires multi-stakeholder collaboration. In this context, stakeholders like regulators and policymakers, business, finance providers, technology innovators, empowered citizens, educational institutions and change managers all play vital roles. They can collectively create the necessary conditions, incentives, paradigms, values, mindsets and cultures that foster effective multi-stakeholder collaboration. By working together, these diverse actors can drive more significant progress towards the crucial task of reinventing critical systems.

This Element explains why business is ideally positioned to lead the multi-stakeholder collaboration for the much-needed transformation of our critical systems. Companies' relationship with society is evolving from one where companies see sustainability challenges as a risk to one where sustainability and systemic transformation are seen as opportunities for new growth. Businesses can convert into transformational organisations by aligning strategic visioning with strengthening of organisational capabilities and development of collaborative networks for impact and new growth.

The paradigm and the mindset out of which a system and its objectives emerge are the strongest potential intervention points for systemic change but also the most challenging ones. This Element describes ten emerging paradigms that will facilitate future-fit systemic change and explores the potential and the dynamics of changing mindsets between corporate and public actors and citizens. Business education can play a critical role in anchoring future-fit paradigms and cultivating the necessary mindset for our future leaders. Leadership skills and tools can be developed that empower leaders to drive change in themselves, their organisations and the systems they are part of. We are convinced that by strengthening skills such as contextual mindfulness, future consciousness, systems range, cross-collaborative competence, radical impact agility and, most importantly, purpose, we can develop a generation of more rounded, humanistic leaders that can lead the transformation to a future of more sustainable and socially just models of value creation within our planetary boundaries.

1 Reinventing Value Creation

Undoubtedly, economic growth driven by shareholder capitalism has catalysed enormous progress worldwide. It has allowed us to feed, house, move and service billions. Nevertheless, the inventor of the modern gross domestic product (GDP) concept in 1934, Simon Kuznets himself, warned that a singular focus on economic growth is too simplistic as it fails to consider the quality and distribution of growth, or the distinction between the short and the long term: 'The welfare of a nation can scarcely be inferred from a measurement of national income' (Kuznets, 1934, p. 7).

Despite Kuznets' warning being often quoted in recent years, and proof stacking up that our current growth model is broken, the addiction to GDP as the ultimate measure of success seems stubbornly hard to shake in economic, business and political circles. The no-brain default solution that most governments and central banks still seem to have for economic slowdown is to boost consumption, increase public spending and lower the cost of credit, incentivising us all to buy 'more stuff we do not need with money we do not have to impress people we do not know', and further driving inequality in the process.

1.1 It's the Economy, Stupid . . . or Is It?

We have entered an era of perverse economic growth. Our current model is increasingly generating economic growth at the expense of natural and social capital. A study by Trucost (2013) concluded that the annual externalities, the cost to natural capital, of our economic activity were $7.3 trillion, roughly 13 per cent of global GDP, with greenhouse gas (GHG) emissions from coal power generation in East Asia and North America, land use from cattle ranching in South America and South Asia, and water use in wheat farming in South Asia topping the list of externalities.

Similarly, Goh, Pfeffer and Zenios (2015) estimated the spending on health care to combat depression and burnout to be more than $190 billion per year in the USA alone. Ironically, this expense resulting from the deterioration of social capital is formally considered a contribution to GDP. Another striking example is the expense of war. Despite often being at the expense of forms of social capital like education or health, the $14 trillion spent by the Pentagon since the start of the Afghan war in 2001 perversely counts towards GDP growth, while the loss of lives and the destruction of assets are not directly accounted for in the GDP calculation (Brown University, 2021).

We need to generate economic well-being, but not at the expense of natural, human and social capital, thus avoiding perverse growth. Anthropogenic climate change, water and resource shortages, biodiversity loss and social inequity, with their interrelations and knock-on effects, significantly impact business and society. In the next ten years, they all pose an enormous threat in terms of both likelihood and impact. According to the *Global Risks Report 2023* by the World Economic Forum (WEF, 2023), eight of the top ten most severe

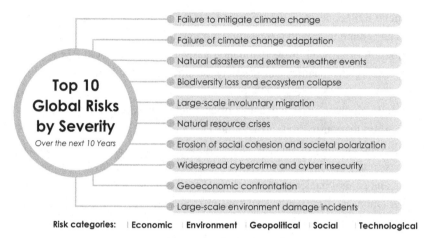

Figure 1 Eight of the biggest global risks in the next ten years are environmental or social.

global risks over the next ten years are environmental and societal (see Figure 1): failure to adapt to and mitigate climate change, natural disasters, biodiversity loss, extreme weather events and ecosystem collapse will directly influence and be influenced by other significant risks identified in the report, such as large-scale involuntary migration, natural resource crises, erosion of social cohesion, geo-economic confrontation and large-scale environmental damage events.

Our obsession with economic GDP has made us collectively lose sight of the fact that, according to the WEF (2020), $44 trillion of economic value generation – more than half of the global GDP – relies moderately or highly on nature and its services, and is therefore exposed to losses of nature. But we extract more natural resources, return more GHG to the air and generate more waste than the earth's natural cycles can compensate for.

We will soon see our GDP growth negatively affected by our failure to act effectively to mitigate climate change. A 2021 analysis of climate and transition risks by the world's largest insurance company, SwissRe, concludes that under the current trajectory, the impacts of climate change are likely to reduce global GDP by 11–14 per cent by 2050 compared to a situation with no climate change (SwissRe, 2021). By comparison, during Covid-19 lockdowns in 2020, global GDP dropped 3.3 per cent. Moreover, because social and environmental issues are so closely related, this also contributes to social injustice and a decline in social capital. Agriculture and natural resources are essential for the survival of three out of every four individuals who live in poverty. Owing to their increased exposure to food and livelihood insecurity, conflict and the health implications of extreme weather events, they are more likely to be disproportionately impacted by climate change.

In an exploratory scenario analysis of the vulnerability and readiness of 135 countries in relation to climate change over the next 30 years, S&P Global Ratings (2022) finds that because lower- and lower-middle-income countries are more exposed to the effects of climate change and have less capacity to adapt, owing to weaker institutions and lower financial capacity, these countries are likely to see 3.6 times more losses on average owing to climate change incidents than higher-middle- and higher-income countries. Swiss Re's (2021) stress tests show that climate change will impact forty-eight countries, representing 90 per cent of the world economy. The disruption and the investment required for economies and societies to adapt are highest in Asia: China is at risk of losing 24 per cent of its GDP without any mitigation actions, while Europe is heading to a loss of 11 per cent and the USA stands to lose close to 10 per cent. Southeast Asia could see GDP reduced by as much as 29 per cent.

Most of our economic growth models are based on material throughput, population growth and the myopic belief that more people producing and consuming more stuff will grow our GDP and, thus, our well-being. Despite history being full of examples of civilisations falling because of living in imbalance with their natural environment (such as the Sumerian, the Mayan and the Angkor civilisations), these last decades we are again learning the hard way that our legacy growth model, too focussed on economic wealth creation alone, is bringing unintended and undesired consequences. Despite having created tremendous economic value, it has become, in many ways, a destructive force, causing climate change and depleting natural capital, promoting short-term wins over long-term prosperity and widening social exclusion. Environmental and social costs, inherent but previously hidden in the old growth model, make it glaringly evident that our old model is unsuitable for the future.

Humanity's biomass accounts for only one ten-thousandth of the life on Earth, measured by the dry weight of carbon that makes up the structure of all living things (Bar-On et al., 2018). However, humans have an enormously outsized influence on all other living things and, because of that, our current pathway looks as follows:

- The human population has grown from 2 billion in the 1920s to more than 8 billion today. Moreover, this trend will only continue, reaching 10 billion people globally in the mid-2050s. Therefore, the biggest challenge of our generation is to satisfy the needs of 8 billion to 10 billion people in ways that do not surpass the environmental limits or erode the social foundations of our societies.

- Climate change is one of the biggest crises the world is currently experiencing. It is accelerating and bringing the world close to irreversible change: out of fifteen climate tipping points identified by the Intergovernmental Panel on Climate Change (IPCC), nine are already at the point of no return, such as the warming of tundras in the northern hemisphere, which is causing a thawing of permafrost, releasing vast amounts of the potent GHG methane into the atmosphere and triggering feedback loops that bring the climate, and us, dangerously close to irreversible tipping points (IPCC, 2020).
- Our global annual burning of fossil fuels is the equivalent of the growth of all plants worldwide for 400 years. Meanwhile, relentless deforestation – the equivalent of one football field every 2 seconds, only half of which is replanted (FAO, 2020) – primarily for agricultural conversion, has turned the Amazon from a carbon sink into a net emitter of GHG.
- We lost two-thirds of the world's animal population in the past fifty years, partly driven by deforestation and by a tenfold increase in the number of dead zones in our oceans owing to agricultural run-off of fertilisers and pesticides (IPBES, 2019). This loss directly affects the robustness of food chains and nature's capacity to defend itself and us against pests and the effects of climate change.
- More extreme weather events caused by climate change will affect food production and livelihoods. The World Bank (2021) predicts 216 million additional climate change migrants by 2050 in Africa, Asia, South America and Eastern Europe alone.
- By 2030, a 40 per cent disparity between water availability and demand is anticipated, and as many as 700 million people could be displaced by water scarcity (HLPW, 2018). Water shortages are predicted to affect one in four people worldwide by 2050, not just in geographies like the Middle East, North Africa and India but also in sections of the USA, Spain and even major cities like London. In addition, water scarcity threatens to push up food costs, which could cause instability and conflict.
- The global economy extracted and used more resources in the past six years than in the entire twentieth century, and levels of waste in our environment have never been higher (CGRI, 2023).
- Only 9 per cent of the 300 million tons of plastics we produce yearly – roughly the equivalent of the weight of the entire human world population combined – is recycled. Most plastics end up in landfill, and an estimated 8 million tons end up in our oceans (WEF et al., 2016). By 2050, more plastic than fish will be in the ocean if the current overfishing and plastic production rate continues.
- Inequality is on the rise. Of all the new wealth in the world, the wealthiest 1 per cent of the world's population on a per-person basis captures more than

110 times the wealth captured by the poorest 50 per cent, who together own just 2 per cent of the world's economic wealth, according to *World Inequality Report 2022* (World Inequality Lab, 2022).

- Covid-19 had a disproportionate impact on poor people. In 2021 alone, 97 million people were pushed back into extreme poverty, bringing the total number of people worldwide living on less than $1.90 per day by the end of 2022 to an estimated 685 million people, according to the World Bank (2022). Moreover, this number might rise further as the knock-on effects of the pandemic (inflation, economic downturn) take shape.

Nature has a remarkable potential to sustain us, whether through the recycling of our water, the digestion of our waste, the production of our food or the removal of CO_2 from the air to create the oxygen we breathe. However, as our species expands, so does our impact. As a result, as man's dominion over nature increases, the capacity of nature to supply its services and to compensate for our impact decreases, exacerbating the effects of our perverse growth and accelerating the 'degeneration' of natural capital. Furthermore, as our natural capital erodes, low-income populations are most heavily affected, widening the gap between rich and poor and eroding the social fabric.

Reason enough to stop and think. Is this the type of economic growth we want? Instead of accelerating our demise, we need to mobilise our innovation and collaboration capacity, not only to reinvent growth to fit within the planet's ecological boundaries and not deteriorate our social foundations but also to regenerate nature's capacity to help us solve our problems and to bolster our social capital through higher levels of inclusion.

1.2 Systemic Challenges Require Systemic Solutions

Most sustainability challenges, such as climate change, waste and resource challenges, natural capital loss, poverty and inequality, are systemic challenges: they involve multiple actors, stakeholders and numerous connected subsystems – social, institutional, cultural, political, economic, technical and ecological – often with governance contexts and dynamics of their own. As a result, these problems are complex, with multiple causal relationships, feedback loops and often unforeseen consequences.

Focussing on individual causal relationships and intervening in just one aspect of these complex systems will almost never solve the problem; rather, it will relocate the problem or cause other unforeseen consequences beyond the causal relationship of focus. Systemic challenges require systemic solutions. This requires a deep understanding of the complex systems surrounding the challenges. Thinking in terms of systems helps us understand the relationships between the components and the actors in a system and foresee the intended and the unintended ripple effects of one's interventions in that system, thus enabling us to envision the most responsible approaches to solving complex societal challenges.

Section 2 will explore system dynamics in more detail, but for a good understanding of our analysis and recommendations, we briefly clarify what we mean by systems, systems thinking and systemic change. Systems thinking expert Donella Meadows defined a system as a set of things – people, cells, molecules or others – interconnected so that they produce their pattern of behaviour over time (Meadows, 1999). Systems exist in the physical world. These can be natural ecosystems, such as the marine environment, and our social systems, such as the food or health-care systems. They can also be socially created systems such as belief systems. When we talk about systems in this Element, we generally refer to the system of actors, conditions and the dynamics between them, and possibly adjacent systems, that have formed around satisfying a societal need, such as societies' need for nutrition, mobility, shelter, health, safety and comfort. These systems are enabled by supporting systems such as finance, energy, education or governance. All these systems involve various smaller parts and organisations at multiple levels that form an intricate whole whose behaviour is influenced by the system's structure, the interaction of its parts and the conditions affecting the system and its parts.

Pioneered by biologists but divided over several disciplines, the main characteristics of systemic thinking or 'thinking in systems' arose in Europe during the 1920s (Capra & Luisi, 2014). These ideas, especially Bertalanffy's concepts of general systems theory and open systems, helped to give birth to a new way of thinking: thinking in terms of patterns, relationships, connectedness and context. The ability to see the interdependence between multiple events happening in different parts of the world, instead of seeing them as isolated events, allows for a richer understanding based on the incorporation of multiple and different (sometimes even conflicting) views. The understanding that 'properties of the parts are not intrinsic properties but can be understood only within the context of the larger whole' was a profound revolution in the history of Western scientific thought. The tremendous shock in twentieth-century science is that 'living systems cannot be understood by analysis' (Capra & Luisi, 2014, p. 66). In contrast to analysis (originating from ancient Greek 'ana' and 'luein', meaning 'loosening up'), in which you take something apart to understand it, system thinking concentrates on putting things in the context of a larger whole. This makes systems thinking contextual, which is the opposite of analytical thinking.

Since the start of the industrial revolution, our focus on growth has led to an ever-thickening web of interdependence worldwide (Senge et al., 2007). At a global scale, cities are connected through investment patterns, consumer choices and international trade. As a result, actions on one side of the planet, which affect supplies ranging from pharmaceuticals to imported staple food, affect livelihoods and employment on the other side of the planet. For example, during the Bangkok floods of 2011, local manufacturing facilities flooded completely and were inoperable for almost two months. As a result, global supply chains for computer and automobile components were severely disrupted, which led to temporary factory closures and lay-offs in many cities outside Thailand (Tyler & Moench, 2012).

The term 'systemic' relies on the concept of elements or components coming together to create a unified whole or a collective of participants. Systemic means 'of or relating to the system' and relates to the complex interactions of multiple actors and conditions in a system. It is often used to describe some phenomenon – an illness, a social problem – that affects every part of an entire system. Of the five interpretations of the word 'systemic' that Midgley and Lindhult (2021) identify, the two dimensions most recently introduced in the literature on systems thinking are 'collaboration' and 'thinking and action'. Collaboration recognises the interdependency of actors in a community or business setting, leading to a need to innovate and co-create value together. In the thinking and action dimension, change is viewed as a process constructed in such a way that 'participants within it use methodologies, methods and techniques to make their thinking and action more systemic' (Midgley & Lindhult, 2021, p. 643). Following these definitions, the term 'systemic change' refers to change involving multiple actors in a system of often interconnected systems, such as social, institutional, cultural, political, economic, technical and ecological systems, as long as it operates in the context of thinking and action towards creating change, which is required when efforts to change one aspect of a system fail to fix the systemic problem.

In the 1980s, prominent American universities and their business schools started focussing on systemic change. It began to gain traction in business and management fields as a way to address the complex and interrelated challenges faced by organisations and society (Bennis & O'Toole, 2005), emphasising the need for a holistic, collaborative and integrated approach to problem-solving rather than relying on isolated or incremental changes. Systemic change affects how the whole system functions (including all its components and relationships), and the change must be fundamental. Moreover, it often changes the system's output (the system-changing impact created).

British plant ecologist Arthur George Tansley coined the term 'ecosystem' in 1935 to characterise animal and plant communities. In 1993, James F. Moore used the biological ecosystem as an analogy to explain business environments and introduced the term 'business ecosystem' (Graça & Camarinha-Matos, 2017). A business ecosystem is 'an economic community supported by a foundation of interacting organisations and individuals – the organisms of the business world. This economic community produces goods and services of value to customers, who themselves are members of the ecosystem' (Graça & Camarinha-Matos, 2017, p. 237). In an interdependent business environment, the business ecosystem actors 'co-evolve their capabilities and roles' (Graça & Camarinha-Matos, 2017, p. 237). A business ecosystem approach allows a vast network of actors to collaborate, build systemic solutions and create holistic ways forward. It represents a new operating logic that is essential to achieving systemic change (Kapetaniou & Rieple, 2017). For some companies, like start-ups, the business ecosystem logic is at the core of business. However, for other companies, a more cooperative and open approach, collective action, bilateral partnerships, holistic thinking, sharing knowledge and capabilities or sharing risks in initial capital investments, and systemic understanding at the individual, organisational and societal levels, are challenges.

1.3 A New Notion of Value

Focussing solely on GDP growth as a measure of value might have seemed reasonable when civilisations were unaware of environmental and social constraints. However, there is ample evidence today that reality is complex and that we must strike a new balance. Our systemic challenges of the climate crisis, natural capital destruction and rising income inequality unfairly impact the bottom of the pyramid, putting pressure on the social contract and risking geopolitical stability while materially impacting business. Whether we believe that policies and regulations should be used to shape new forms of production and consumption, or that new technologies will magically solve all our problems (tech utopianism), our growth model and definition of value need to be revised for the societal and environmental realities of the twenty-first century. There is a need for a new growth model that works with nature rather than against it, that emphasises well-being in the longer term rather than the short, and that encompasses everyone rather than just a fortunate few.

Business leaders and academic experts have developed various models to redefine value. While a sustainability transformation is underway, challenges and resistances remain. Nevertheless, there are currently five leading value-creation concepts that reconceive business's value to society (Weenk & Henzen, 2021):

1. **Stakeholder Value**: Central to this concept is how stakeholders work cooperatively to create value through a set of relations among specific groups that have a stake in the activities and outcomes of the business and upon whom the business depends for achieving its objectives.
2. **Blended Value**: In this conceptual framework, businesses, investments and non-profit organisations are evaluated based on their ability to generate a blend of social, environmental and financial value. This holistic approach is sometimes used interchangeably with the triple bottom line's people, profit and planet.
3. **Shared Value**: In this framework, a business's success and social progress are interdependent. It enhances a business's competitiveness while advancing the economic and social conditions of the communities in which it operates.
4. **Sustainable Value**: The framework views global sustainability challenges through the business lens, which helps identify the right practices and strategies to contribute to a more sustainable world, while simultaneously driving shareholder value.
5. **Integrated Value**: This relates to the simultaneous building of multiple 'non-financial' capitals, such as human, ecological, social, technological and infrastructural capital, through synergistic innovation across the nexus economy (including the circular, well-being, access, exponential and resilience economies), that results in net-positive effects, thus making our world more satisfying, sustainable, shared, smart and secure.

As awareness of our need to find new value-creation models grows, paradigms shift. New growth concepts and paradigms are emerging around these new notions of value. In 2004, Wen Jiabao, the Chinese premier, had ambitions for a green GDP index to replace the Chinese GDP index as a performance measure: green gross domestic product (GGDP) is a measure of economic growth with environmental consequences (degradation, resource depletion, cost of protection and restoration) of that growth factored into a country's conventional GDP. But, in 2006, the first GGDP accounting report showed that the financial loss caused by pollution was $66 billion, or 3 per cent of China's economy (China Dialogue, 2006). As the adjustment for environmental damage would reduce the growth rate to politically unacceptable levels, nearly zero in some provinces, the government withdrew its support for the GGDP methodology the following year. However, in China's recent push for greener development, experts have argued for the return of GGDP, and China's Five-Year Plans now explicitly make local governments accountable for environmental quality and ecological conservation (Wang, 2016).

Like the leading value-creating concepts or the GGDP, more concepts recognise natural and social capital alongside economic capital as sources of value and well-being. In the same way that an investment in economic capital, such as production capacity or financial assets, can yield economic profits, natural capital (the stock of biomass, biodiversity or natural resources in sustainable natural cycles) produces value in the form of natural services, such as clean water, clean air, food, natural resources and medicine (almost half of our medicines originate in nature) or even recreation space (Wong, 2001). Moreover, societies with high social capital, referring to the extent to which individuals are educated, physically and mentally healthy and part of a safe, transparent and inclusive society, yield trusted, collaborative relationships that are much more productive than societies with lower levels of social capital.

Recognition of social and natural capital alongside economic capital gives rise to new ways of framing and calculating growth. The concept of Gross National Happiness, pioneered by the Bhutan government, inspired Jeffrey Sachs at the Sustainable Development Solutions Network (SDSN) to develop the World Happiness Report. It ranks countries based on a mix of criteria, including GDP per capita, social support, life expectancy, freedom to make choices, generosity and perception of corruption. Even though the economic picture is uneven across Europe, the democracies of continental northern Europe provide interesting learning on how highly transparent, egalitarian, inclusive societies that value natural and social capital alongside economic capital consistently rank among the world's happiest countries. Finland, Iceland, Denmark, the Netherlands, Sweden and Norway ranked among the World Happiness top eight every year from 2019 to 2022 (Helliwell et al., 2022).

The triple bottom line concept of 'people, profit and planet' has evolved into frameworks that aim to optimise value creation within planetary and social boundaries. Doughnut Economics, championed by Kate Raworth (2017), identifies the space in which humanity can optimise its well-being, while making sure not to break through the social foundations of individuals' equal and fundamental rights to education, health, justice, housing, energy, food and income or to exceed the ecological boundaries for factors such as biodiversity loss, air pollution, freshwater withdrawals, land conversion or climate change. The City of Amsterdam (2020) in the Netherlands is the first city to adopt the Doughnut Economics model to inform city-wide strategies and developments to provide a good quality of life for everyone without putting additional pressure on the planet.

A more constructive focus on the shared value potential is provided through the concepts of regenerative and inclusive growth, which aim to restore natural and social capital and resilience while being economically sustainable.

Originally applied mainly in agriculture, regenerative business practices are entering other sectors such as tourism, medicine and consumer goods. For example, Danone (2017) is teaching and incentivising regenerative practices to farmers in its supply chain and frames it as a crucial part of its commitment to become water impact positive and achieve net zero emissions by 2050. At a global level, the Bonn Challenge (2011) has already mobilised commitments from sixty countries in the last decade to restore 210 million hectares of degraded and deforested land. Even though the commitments are numerical, and the quality of reforestation remains an issue, the challenge is on track towards bringing 350 million hectares into restoration by 2030.

Nature-based solutions (NBS) are based on the realisation that nature can be our biggest ally. Restoring or leveraging nature's ability to provide its services can yield substantial economic, environmental and health benefits. For example, knowing the potentially disastrous impact of their activity on coastal ecosystems, several oil companies around the world have started investing in mangrove restoration projects. The high carbon-sequestration potential of mangroves, removing up to four times more CO_2 from the air than mature tropical forests, contribute to these companies reaching their carbon reduction targets while providing essential benefits to coastal communities through increased biodiversity, fishery nurseries and coastal protection. Another example of cost-effectively harnessing nature is how New York City achieves some of the cleanest drinking water of any city in the world (Hu, 2018). By investing $1.7 billion since the early 1990s in conserving 400,000 hectares of the upstream watershed and letting nature filter its drinking water, the city has avoided building a massive $10 billion filtration plant and is saving at least another $100 million annually on its operation.

Especially when dealing with environmental challenges, through hundreds of millions of years of evolution, nature harbours enormous wisdom and potential solutions to our problems. As explored in Janine Benyus's (2002) work, biomimicry is the design and production of structures, systems and materials modelled on biological entities and processes. In addition to us sourcing medicines from nature, the fascinating discipline of biomimicry has inspired multiple innovations, such as:

- reverse osmosis membrane filtering technology that is used for water purification and desalination and that mimics how the roots of mangrove trees separate salt from seawater;
- water harvesting from the air, already deployed as an essential solution to water scarcity in places like Ethiopia and Chile, that was inspired by Stenocara beetles surviving in dry climates;

- the growing application of passive cooling techniques in architecture, inspired by African termites drilling tiny holes to stimulate airflow to cool down their mounds;
- the development of nano-paints, inspired by the skin of sharks and lotus flowers, that reduce water resistance and increase ships' speed and energy efficiency.

Many new business models are emerging to achieve growth on a finite planet, decoupling economic growth from material use and focussing on satisfying needs rather than providing goods, thus dematerialising growth. The sharing economy, or collaborative consumption, aims to minimise material use per unit of customer satisfaction by optimising the usage of existing stock and infrastructure. For example, there are approximately 1.45 billion vehicles worldwide, of which about 1.1 billion are passenger cars. However, the average car is parked for 23 hours daily and is highly inefficient as less than 1 per cent of total life-cycle energy input is used to move a person (Nagler, 2021). Carpooling or car-sharing schemes, like ZipCar, Lyft or Uber, address this radical inefficiency. This economic model has already disrupted several industries, especially asset-intensive ones like transportation and hospitality. Despite this collaborative consumption model having taken a hit during the Covid-19 pandemic, analysts forecast that it will continue making inroads into the consumer goods, media and entertainment, and health-care sectors and grow more than fivefold to $335 billion by 2025 (PwC, 2015).

Anything-as-a-service (XaaS) also addresses this efficiency challenge, especially in fast-changing sectors such as information technology (IT), by offering products, tools and technologies as a service over a network instead of on-site locally. The XaaS models are expected to grow by 19 per cent annually between 2022 and 2028, reaching a $1.6 trillion market share by 2028 (KBV Research, 2022). For example, Signify, formerly Philips Lighting, offers lighting-as-a-service to its public sector and commercial customers. The customers pay a monthly service fee for light; in turn, Signify installs, operates and maintains the lighting systems. These systems are designed for easy replacement and repair during operational life, and, in the after-use stage, they can be easily reused or recycled. Signify reports multiple benefits of its XaaS model, such as a 75 per cent longer lifespan, a reduction in energy consumption, and a significant emissions and energy reduction compared to its conventional counterparts (Ellen MacArthur Foundation, 2023).

In 2012, a Google search for 'circular economy' yielded 22,600 results; that exact same search today leads to more than 190 million hits. The primary schools of thought related to circular economy are performance economy, biomimicry, blue economy, regenerative design and cradle-to-cradle. The last one, in particular, is seen as a conceptual breakthrough in the maturity of circularity, but circularity itself is nothing new: between the 1970s and the 1990s, it focussed mainly on dealing with waste; from the 1990s to 2010 the focus lay on connecting input and output in strategies for eco-efficiency; currently, circularity focusses on maximising value retention in the age of resource depletion, having introduced the 10 R strategy framework of Remine, Recover, Recycle, Repurpose, Remanufacture, Refurbish, Repair, Resell/Reuse, Reduce and Refuse (Reike et al., 2018). The circular economy model focusses not just on eliminating pollution and waste, circulating materials and products for as long as possible or dematerialising consumption, but also on regenerating nature in an economic system that benefits businesses, people and the natural world equally. Shanghai-based company Waste2Wear is an excellent example of adopting the circular economy model. It produces 100 per cent RPET (recycled polyethene terephthalate) from pre-ocean and pre-landfill plastic bottles and RPP (recycled polypropylene) from end-of-life single-use food containers and domestic appliances and turns that into yarn, fabrics and other finished products. On top of this, it has also introduced an award-winning sustainable supply chain management system that is verified by blockchain technology (Waste2Wear, n.d.).

Dematerialisation models such as XaaS, the sharing economy and the circular economy can be very successful due to lower per-unit footprint and cost. However, the dirty not-so-little secret of these models might be harder to address. As things become cleaner and cheaper, we tend to use more of them, diminishing the beneficial effects of the new technology or measure. This is called the rebound effect. For example, while XaaS brings down the per-unit environmental footprint of IT solutions, the rebound effect of the increased overall consumption of cloud-based services because of increased accessibility is causing the industry's overall environmental footprint to boom. Global internet traffic has increased twentyfold since 2010, and data centres and transmission networks today consume 2–3 per cent of the world's electricity, which is more than the entire global aviation industry (International Energy Agency, 2022). The impact is expected to continue to grow in the decade ahead, despite data service providers setting up centres in cold climate regions with high availability of renewable energy, such as the Scandinavian Arctic Circle and Iceland.

Shifting our focus of intervention, can we help societies be happier and healthier by encouraging and providing more mental rather than material growth? Without denying consumerism, brand builders are perfectly equipped to optimise the intangible attributes in their product development and marketing, thus 'dematerialising' consumption without diminishing perceived value. For example, Japanese culinary culture carries some of this philosophy, mastering the art of serving one strawberry for dessert as the minimalist climax of a special dinner.

1.4 Change in a VUCA World

Change is accelerating. In the early twentieth century, it took 75 years for the telephone to scale to 100 million users. Mobile phones took 16 years, Facebook 4.5 years, Instagram 2.5 years, TikTok 9 months and ChatGPT amassed more than 100 million users within 2 months of its launch in November 2022 (Milmo, 2023). The emergence of disruptive and exponential business models in a hyper-connected, increasingly digital world is leading corporate and individual fortunes to be made and lost quicker than ever. For example, 52 per cent of the companies listed in the Fortune 500 in 2000 no longer exist today. Within one generation, Jeff Bezos and Elon Musk, founders of Amazon (1994) and Tesla (2003), respectively, became the wealthiest people on the planet. Today's average tenure of an S&P500 company is less than twenty years, down from sixty years in the 1950s (Capgemini Consulting, 2015).

Digital hyper-connectedness can be a force for good, as we have seen in Ukrainian citizens connecting and coordinating their efforts to defend themselves against the 2022 Russian invasion. However, it can also be a destabilising factor. Impulsive, indiscriminate sharing helps sensationalist fake news spread online, contributing to the algorithms embedded in many social media feeds polarising rather than uniting society. As a result, free speech has come under discussion, and not only authoritarian governments are responding with stricter internet controls.

So-called black swan events are on the rise. But these surprises might not be entirely unexpected if we look at the bigger picture. As humanity continues to destroy biodiversity and heat the planet, we also deplete nature's ability to provide natural protection against extreme weather events and pests or viruses like bird flu or Covid-19. Recent events showed how sensitive to disruption most industries' supply chains are. Many governments are defaulting to responding to crises by injecting enormous financial recovery packages into the economy. However, as the world rebounds from the pandemic, supply shortages in, for example, fossil fuels, compounded by the impacts of the Ukraine war, translating into inflation levels not seen in most parts of the world in forty years. This uncertainty is made investors nervous, thus pushing up volatility in the stock markets. The S&P500 index in 2022 showed a level of volatility not seen since the financial crisis of 2008.

Being a world population that is growing exponentially on a finite planet requires us to urgently and radically reinvent how we produce and consume if we are to remain within the Earth's sustainable boundaries. Nevertheless, despite progress over the last decades, mainly thanks to China's spectacular achievement of lifting 770 million of its people out of poverty in the last 40 years, in 2022 almost half of the global population still lived in poverty, making less than $7 per day, a number that could rise further due to the compounded effects of Covid-19 and the Ukraine war, according to the World Bank (2022). This is forcing us to confront the ambiguous challenge of dematerialising the consumption of a growing world population while finding ways to provide affordable and accessible energy, health care, nutrition and basic opportunities for the less fortunate members of our societies.

Complex societal issues like the climate crisis, inequality, biodiversity loss and natural capital degradation can no longer be ignored. The anticipated costs and impacts of anthropogenic climate change are enormous. The United Nations Environment Programme has estimated that the global cost of adapting to the impacts of climate change is expected to grow to $140 billion–$300 billion per year by 2030 and to $280 billion–$500 billion per year by 2050 (United Nations Environment Programme, 2021). This has forcefully motivated nations, cities and companies worldwide to commit to radical reductions in GHG emissions. As of early 2023, more than 132 national governments have made net zero commitments. In addition, more than 11,000 non-state actors, including 8,300 companies and more than 1,100 cities, have also made net zero commitments as part of the United Nations Race To Zero (United Nations Climate Change, n.d.). This will require a radical reinvention of how we produce, distribute and consume, affecting virtually all industries, supply chains and geographies worldwide.

In this VUCA reality, companies need to reinvent themselves and the systems they are part of. However, VUCA means that it is increasingly hard to understand and predict the future and the outcomes of one's actions. Strategies can no longer be based on extrapolating existing situations and legacy business models but must increasingly lean on the agile pursuit of a compelling vision supported by multiple stakeholders. Nevertheless, due to exponential technological progress and the size of our impact (compare a train derailing at 30 kilometres/hour in the early 1800s to one derailing at 300 kilometres/hour today), the stakes are too high to continue progressing through trial and error. Our imperative to achieve change in a VUCA world increases the importance of a specific set of future-fit leadership skills and the ability to collaborate, which we discuss in Section 3.

Box 1 How Does VUCA Affect Change Processes and Willingness to Change?

For one thing, VUCA calls into question the applicability of traditional change management models such as Lewin's U-model, Kotter's 8 Steps, and Design Thinking. These have already received criticism for paying too little attention to the most challenging aspect of the change process: actual adoption by its stakeholders. A VUCA world amplifies what Herbert Simon (1957) described as bounded rationality, that is, people having limited information and lacking the attention spans and computational capacity to digest the complexity they are faced with, limiting their ability to take rational decisions as assumed in neoclassical economics.

Understanding the irrationality of decision-makers via the lens of behavioural science can be helpful. In a VUCA environment, these irrational aspects of human nature, which include a tendency to reject change and avoid uncertainty, memory distortion, poor prognostication of future behaviour, and vulnerability to physical and emotional states, tend to become more pronounced. When trying to convince stakeholders to collaborate, it is helpful to consider and influence both the fast, automatic and subconscious decision-making process, as described by Kahneman (2011), and the slow, deliberate and conscious process. It is also vital to become more deliberate in framing situations, options and decisions in ways tailored to the various stakeholders' values and preferred languages.

Uncertainty and volatility are associated with higher risk. As people are naturally certainty-seeking, uncertainty usually induces them to act in ways that reduce uncertainty, such as by seeking information. However, in a VUCA world, uncertainty and ambiguity are the norms: priorities change, information is unreliable and results are difficult to predict. If new information is unclear or ambiguous, information overload and paralysis-by-analysis may happen. Moreover, ambiguity hinders decision-making; this is not conducive to any kind of change, let alone systemic change. Nevertheless, research has shown that it rather is attitude towards ambiguity that is a robust predictor of willingness to engage in costly social behaviour to enrich a shared knowledge base and build a shared understanding and vision that can support decisions and actions (Vives & FeldmanHall, 2018).

1.5 We Are Running Out of Time

In the early 1970s, Paul Ehrlich and John Holdren developed and popularised the IPAT equation to describe how humanity's impact (I) on the

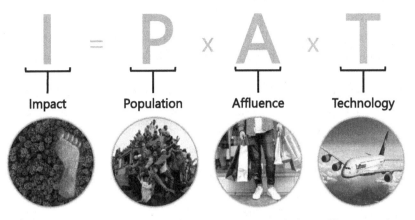

Figure 2 Humanity's impact is a function of population, affluence and technology.

planet is a function of population size (P), affluence (A) and technology (T) (see Figure 2) (Holdren, 2018).

Population growth has not helped to lessen the human impact. A hundred years ago, a newborn would have come into a world with fewer than 2 billion people. The number of people on our globe exceeded 8 billion in November 2022 (The World Counts, 2023). Although relative growth has slowed significantly, the population of the globe continues to rise by 200,000 people every single day. Affluence, the amount of consumption per person, if reflected as a measure of per capita GDP, albeit spread unevenly, has more than tripled worldwide in the last thirty years (World Bank, 2023). This puts all our hopes on technology. Tech-utopianists will argue that technology is a powerful force that has brought tremendous progress in many ways, and they trust that technological innovations will solve humanity's problems (Hickman & Banister, 2009). However, they frequently overlook three crucial elements that have caused impact to rise far more quickly than it has fallen as a result of improved technology:

1. **The rebound effect**: As described in Section 1.3, price reductions brought on by efficiency incline us to consume more of what we intended to conserve. As air conditioners become more efficient, we install more of them. As flying has become cheaper in the last fifteen years, the number of miles travelled has more than doubled.

2. **The unintended consequences of technological advancement**: The promise of positive features frequently causes us to overlook the potential negative impact of innovations. Examples are when new technology, such as 5G, exacerbates inequality because the investment required to provide the

technology is feasible only in rich and densely populated geographies, or the way social media not only connects people but also facilitates the spread of misinformation, not to mention the impact it has on the psychological well-being of many users.

3. **Politics and vested interests**: Even though money is available to address issues like poverty, climate change and pollution, the adoption of technological innovations frequently slows down due to opposed political ideologies or the influence and interests of legacy industries, such as the fossil fuel industry.

Given the dramatic and unfavourable trend of the components making up the above formula, the world must catch up on almost all of the United Nations SDGs. According to the latest SDG Report (United Nations, 2022b), significant challenges remain for most SDG indicators, especially in low-to-medium-income countries. As of 2023, only 18 per cent of the SDG targets are on track, with most facing serious challenges and 15 per cent of SDG targets, including those on hunger, poverty and CO2 reversing (Sustainable Development Report, 2022). According to the United Nations Framework Convention on Climate Change (2016), by 2030, GHG emissions must be reduced by 45 per cent from 2010 to prevent global warming from reaching uncontrollable levels. All national action plans together, however, might not be enough: taking all national action plans as of October 2022 into account, in the upcoming eight years, emissions are still anticipated to climb by 10 per cent (United Nations, 2022a). Moreover, in its latest update of March 2023, the IPCC (2023) concludes that there are significant delays in implementing the national action plans; these are pushing the Paris goal of limiting global warming to 1.5°C out of reach. The IPCC is instead projecting that without strengthening policies, an increase of 3.2°C by the end of the century is very likely.

We are running out of time for marginal, incremental improvements. It is crucial to recognise when incremental change is insufficient for achieving desired objectives; now, revolutionary change must be attempted (Kenny & Meadowcroft, 1999; Kates et al., 2012). In its climate report on impact, adaptation and vulnerability, the IPCC (2022) warns that transformational change is no longer optional; it is necessary. To keep the possibility alive of us living within the planet's natural boundaries in socially just ways, we must dramatically accelerate the sustainability transition and radically improve the sustainability of some of the most critical systems that support us, such as the food, energy, transport and infrastructure systems. Furthermore, we must rethink critical enabling systems such as financial, urban, educational and social systems.

Governments are committing trillions to support mitigation and transformation efforts over the coming decades. Sustainability is not a 'nice to have'; it is critical and urgent if we want to avoid the disruptions and the dramatic costs to natural and social capital that are escalating under our business-as-usual model. We need radical reinvention, not marginal or incremental change of our systems. Radical, from the Latin 'radix', means 'at the roots', not shallow or superficial. The societal need to mitigate and adapt to the effects of climate change and natural capital loss and to radically reinvent our systems is the biggest challenge and the most prominent commercial opportunity of this generation.

The order is tall. And the tension is rising. Many of our current critical systems are not fit for the future and need to be reinvented. But systemic change is hard and complex; we are running out of time and the context is more VUCA than ever. This is why we need a better understanding of how systems work and how we can create the conditions and equip our decision-makers to achieve systemic change.

2 Where to Intervene?

Think of any complex value chain or system as a game of Jenga: removing or replacing one block could disrupt the whole and influence all the other blocks (see Figure 3). By focussing on entire systems and their many interrelated parts, we can better understand how our decisions affect social, economic and eco-logical problems and identify the opportunities for innovation and intervention that will help us achieve our larger systemic goals.

To transition on time to the more sustainable models the world needs, we need to organise and equip ourselves to radically reinvent some of our critical

Figure 3 A game of Jenga resembling a system: remove, replace and disrupt.

systems. Instead of minor tweaks and incremental change, the focus needs to be on radical departures from the status quo to shift our current unsustainable trajectory to one where normative goals for sustainability are achieved, and political and economic power structures deliver the common good (McPhearson et al., 2021). However, how can we stimulate and deliberately steer systemic change, given the challenges described?

2.1 The WHAT, HOW and WHY of Systemic Change

The USA and the EU have launched projects of unprecedented ambition in response to climate change. The US Senate approved a $369 billion climate budget, aiming to halve US carbon emissions by 2030 from 2005 levels (Morgan, 2022). The EU is backing up its Green Deal with various funding mechanisms worth more than €1 trillion, including a Climate Action Fund and a Just Transition Mechanism, with the objective to make the world's third-largest economy climate-neutral by 2050 (EUcalls, 2022). In the Asia-Pacific region, a study by PwC (2022a) forecasts sustainability assets under management to triple to $3.3 trillion between 2021 and 2026, showing that this part of the world is quickly joining the race to create more sustainable models.

Transformation sometimes requires an upfront investment; therefore, financial and regulatory support in the early phases is vital to de-risk investments for the private sector and accelerate the development of new solutions. However, it is not the amount of money pledged that guarantees successful systemic change. The question remains where and how to invest the resources. Which intervention areas will most effectively drive systemic change?

To illustrate that intervention points are often counter-intuitive, system thinking expert Donella Meadows (1999) often uses economic growth as an example: 'Growth has costs as well as benefits, but we typically do not count the costs – among which are poverty and hunger, environmental destruction, and so on – the whole list of problems we are trying to solve with growth! What is needed is much slower growth and, in some cases, no growth or negative growth' (p. 1). She states that vision without action is useless, but 'action without vision does not know where to go or why to go there. Therefore, vision is necessary to guide and motivate action. More than that, when widely shared and firmly kept in sight, vision brings into being new systems' (Meadows et al., 1992, p. 224).

To synthesise Meadows' (1999) original intervention points for systemic change, and create a practical translation for the business community, we have categorised these levers into the WHAT, HOW and WHY of systemic change in increasing order of transformational potential (see Figure 4).

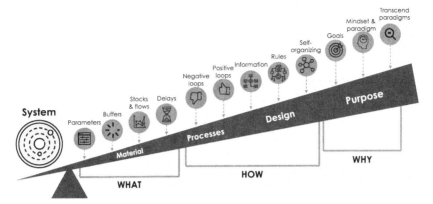

Figure 4 Levers for systemic change.

2.1.1 WHAT: The Conditions of the System

Tweaking parameters, such as price subsidies, minimum wages, bank reserves, taxes and funding models for transition risk-sharing, can all improve systemic change conditions (see Table 1). However, these levers can be categorised as shallow or low potential intervention points (Meadows, 1999). Changing a system's parameters can help a system find a new balance, but systemic change will often be limited unless supported by and coherent with a new mindset and objectives. For example, a one-off windfall tax or increased capital gains taxes for the wealthy, as discussed following the Covid-19 pandemic to address income inequality, will not change the system if the system is still designed to have economic gains flow towards capital providers. It will likely only motivate the wealthy to find new ways to avoid taxes. Similarly, setting a minimum quota for women on an executive team will not solve gender inequality unless efforts are made to improve women's access to relevant, quality education and change corporate mindsets regarding equal opportunities and participation.

2.1.2 HOW: The Dynamics of the System

A more powerful lever over the performance (see Table 2) of a system is the ability of actors to influence the rules of the system, for example through incentives, punishments and constraints, or its structure, for example through the strengthening of positive or negative feedback loops. This ability is strengthened through improved information flows to and engagement of relevant stakeholders and a fair distribution of power. A simple intervention in the flow of information – adding a new loop of information – causes people to behave differently. For example, sustainable food labelling and certification have increased consumer

Table 1 Overview of the WHAT of interventions.

Intervention area	Realm of leverage	Leverage point	Example
WHAT	Material	Constants, parameters, or numbers	Price subsidies, minimum wage, emission standards, the average fuel consumption of a car, or environmental standards. People care about these, but they rarely change behaviour: these interventions will not kick-start systemic change and often have unintended consequences
	Material	The sizes of buffers and other stabilising stocks, relative to their flows	Bank reserves, water reservoirs, total amount of standing timber in a production forest, or just-in-time inventories. A system can be stabilised by increasing the buffer, but when the buffer becomes too big, it counteracts and the system becomes inflexible
	Material	Structure of material stocks, flows and their physical arrangement	Transport networks, plumbing structure, the population age structure, or water drainage systems. This leverage point is rarely simple because the design of the physical structure has often already been laid out and is hard to change
	Process	Lengths of delays, relative to rate systemic change, that causes systems to over-or undershoot	The construction of a new powerplant and the change in demand during its whole lifespan, or the time it takes for the ozone hole to close after harmful emissions seize

Table 2 Overview of the HOW of interventions.

Intervention area	Realm of leverage	Leverage point	Example
HOW	Process	Strength of negative feedback loop, relative to impact (positive feedback loop) they are correcting	To keep a system within safe bounds, humans create negative feedback loops and in nature they evolve (self-correcting): internalising external costs, pollution tax, impact fees, or the extent to which a lake can absorb nutrients and remain clear
	Process	The fine-tuning of positive, self-reinforcing feedback loops	Positive feedback loops are sources of growth, explosion, erosion or collapse. An unchecked positive loop will ultimately destroy its system (e.g. the more the soil erodes, the fewer crops it supports, the fewer roots and leaves to soften rain, so the soil erodes further). Instead of introducing negative loops, it is more effective to weaken and slow the positive loop by introducing progressive income tax, inheritance tax, universal high-quality public education, or green bonds
	Design	Structure of information flow (who has and does not have access to information)	Transparency, crowd-sourcing, or the democratisation of information, such as providing consumers with knowledge about where certain products come from to make informed decisions
	Design	The rules of the system, such as incentives, punishments, or constraints	Policies to level the playing field, governing natural resources, incl. taxes and regulations, such as lowering taxes on the repair of household goods to extend lifespan, reducing CO_2 emissions or addressing the current disposal and replacement culture
	Design	Power to change, add, evolve, or self-organise a system structure	Ability of farmers to organise the sustainable use of communal pasture to improve soil quality for the whole community; or workers union representatives on a corporate board

awareness. They are driving consumer behaviour change, as well as collaboration and cooperation among different actors in the food value chain (Swinnen & Kuijpers, 2019). Similarly, extended mandatory guarantee periods on appliances are proving to slow down the buy-use-replace feedback loop, boosting local repair and recycling business sectors and radically reducing waste in the system. The systemic change potential of these medium-potential levers is enhanced if the actors and stakeholders in the system share the same paradigm, mindset, purpose and vision.

2.1.3 WHY: The Purpose of the System

The most powerful, deep leverage points for systemic change are related to the intent and purpose of the system: What human or social need is the system aiming to satisfy? What type of world is the system aiming to build? In practical terms, this refers to the objectives set for the new system, the values and mindset from which the new system emerges and the ability to transcend existing paradigms (see Table 3). Kramer et al. (2018) have also underlined the importance of mental models as highest potential intervention points from which to change systems. They argue that due to the interdependent nature of the other conditions of systems change (which they identify as relationships and connections, power dynamics, policies, practices and resource flows), intervening in these deep WHY leverage points should be supported by consistent interventions in the shallower HOW and WHAT leverage points. For example, to create a world in which protecting or restoring natural capital is critical and where the objective is to dematerialise, that is, decouple economic growth from resource use, taxing critical resource use could make more sense than taxing income.

We want to suggest a refinement of Meadows' original categorisation of subsidies as a shallow WHAT lever. Direct price subsidies could be considered shallow as they have the side-effect of distorting market mechanisms. However, while market mechanisms ideally need a level playing field to function optimally, policymakers realise that significant transformations require support in the upfront investment required to develop and scale new solutions. Subsidies have the potential to enable Moore's law, accelerating the learning and cost curves, thus facilitating the scaling of new technologies far beyond where they would have scaled without subsidies, which might turn out to be crucial in a world that urgently needs radical change (Wessner, 2003).

The direct industry and technology subsidies provided by China and the USA, such as those announced under the $369 billion Inflation Reduction Act, are putting pressure on Europe, which so far has been trying to steer clear of direct subsidies, to join the clean tech subsidy race. However, acknowledging the

Table 3 Overview of the WHY of interventions.

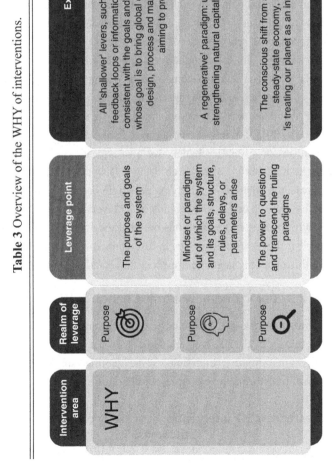

Intervention area	Realm of leverage	Leverage point	Example
WHY	Purpose	The purpose and goals of the system	All 'shallower' levers, such as physical flows and stocks, feedback loops or information flows, should be pivoted to be consistent with the goals and purpose of the system. A system whose goal is to bring global equity will have markedly different design, process and material features than a system aiming to promote free trade
	Purpose	Mindset or paradigm out of which the system and its goals, structure, rules, delays, or parameters arise	A 'regenerative' paradigm: underpinning agricultural policies, strengthening natural capital and supporting social foundations
	Purpose	The power to question and transcend the ruling paradigms	The conscious shift from a growth-based economy to a steady-state economy, such as asking the question 'is treating our planet as an infinite resource good for mankind?'

potential of subsidising research, development and innovation (RD&I), such as through Horizon Europe, the European Commission in late 2022 adopted amendments to the state aid framework that make it easier for member states to access Green Deal funds to financially support RD&I activities to accelerate the green and digital transitions (Allenbach-Ammann, 2022). Leveraging public funding to mobilise private RD&I funding and, more powerfully, facilitate RD&I platforms and ecosystems will accelerate the learning feedback loop, amplify information flows and allow more actors to participate in innovating the processes and design aspects of a system. Subsidising RD&I efforts could therefore be seen as a medium-potential HOW lever.

Mazzucato (2018) is a strong voice in favour of mission-oriented research and innovation (R&I), demonstrating how public expenditure can de facto operate as an industrial policy by addressing grand societal challenges such as climate change. Mowery (2012) argues that lessons from the government's mission-oriented research and development (R&D) spending on national defence, for example, could be applied to society's grand challenges. Defence R&D spending changed many systems beyond defence, facilitating the development of solutions as wide-ranging as the Internet, the Global Positioning System (GPS), radar, virtual reality and even feminine hygiene products (Frohlich et al., 2019). While we acknowledge the subsidising of RD&I as a potential lever for systemic change, we also want to recognise the risk of biases and the malleability of research design. History is full of examples of subsidised research where the underlying paradigm or mindset of the sponsors influenced the research design and conclusions. Players in the tobacco, meat and oil sectors have been spending millions on what they call a balanced scientific approach; what they are referring to, in less euphemistic terms, is sponsored research to downplay the negative impacts of their industries (Keane, 2020).

2.2 Lessons from Systemic Change in Practice

In their literature review of 301 articles on interventions in the food and energy systems, Dorninger et al. (2020) concluded that 80 per cent of interventions are not explicitly transformative (or systemic). We identified six key learnings from our analysis of transformation examples and literature:

1 WHAT without WHY interventions are likely to deliver suboptimal outcomes.

In our efforts to create the right conditions to enable deliberate transformation to emerge from complex systems dynamics, there is currently a disproportionate focus on parameter interventions, the WHAT realm, advocating for leveraging existing mechanisms such as setting targets, introducing standards or providing subsidies, but falling short on developing new processes or rethinking existing ones as a prerequisite for achieving system-changing outcomes. Moreover, a singular focus on parameter interventions poses a risk of creating interventions that lack the interrogation of the dominant worldview, values and paradigms that underpin the current system (Angheloiu & Tennant, 2020).

Shallow levers can potentially support systemic change, but shallow interventions may backfire in the absence of a suitable paradigm or shared mindset on the part of the stakeholders. This became clear when the French government's decision to increase taxes on fossil fuels resulted in the violent 'yellow jackets' protests that eventually forced the government to revert its decision. Similar reactions followed the Dutch government's efforts to curb Dutch farming's nitrogen footprint by imposing limits and standards on agricultural activity without giving enough attention to building a shared understanding and mindset with the Dutch farmers and the public. Another, more corrosive way of backfiring is that interventions in the low-potential-parameter realm invite greenwashing or outright cheating. For example, while it lacks the adequate paradigm, the car industry has a very significant role in fighting climate change; yet, in 2015, decision-makers at Volkswagen and other car manufacturers decided to respond to emissions standards by cheating on diesel emissions tests. This 'Dieselgate' scandal eventually caused the entire board of Volkswagen to be replaced and cost the company more than $33 billion in fines, settlements and expenses. At least this feedback loop was still functioning.

2 Lack of alignment between subsystems hinders systemic change.

Governance contexts, such as those of actors and subsystems, fragmented institutional arrangements, contested policy processes and tightly constrained or poorly delineated roles and capabilities of policymakers and administrators, complicate collaboration for change at a systemic level (Geels, 2005; Smith & Stirling, 2005). Creating systemic change requires a comprehensive approach that considers multiple policy and regulation perspectives. A narrow focus on problem-solving seems to lead to sectoral solutions, often developed in silos that tend to maintain the status quo, while missing opportunities for larger systemic changes (Hynes et al., 2020) and lacking consideration of planetary justice and global democracy (Biermann, 2021). Even well-intentioned legislation aimed at prevention has yet to be successful in avoiding unintended consequences (Hunt et al., 2020). A lack of shared vision and understanding of the interdependencies within the more extensive system has been complicating India's challenge to overcome conflicts among its environmental, poverty, energy and agricultural policies for decades. Efforts to support poor smallholder farmers were negatively affecting the food system in India, as heavy subsidising of electricity, water and fertilisers instead of investment in R&D and capacity building resulted in groundwater depletion, soil deterioration and eutrophication of water bodies, while the state controls over pricing and distribution complicated the creation of additional routes to market despite higher production (World Bank, 2012). Countries like Norway and Finland have found ways to achieve more-joined-up policies for public health and a sustainable food supply by, for example, introducing a national food policy council to provide integrated policy advice (Barling et al., 2002).

Another example of co-evolution and interdependency is the development of hydrogen. Even though 200 years old, hydrogen holds excellent promise as a clean power technology. However, its viability as a low-carbon option largely depends on access to cheap renewable energy being scaled cost-effectively (Baykara, 2018). Collaborating with multiple actors across the car manufacturing value chain allows Swedish H2 Green Steel to scale up its hydrogen-powered production of green steel in northern Sweden, where cheap, clean and abundant hydro-power can be used to produce hydrogen. However, against a backdrop of a forecast rise in demand for steel by more than one-third by 2050 and the need to reduce overall CO_2 emissions by 50 per cent over the same period, this begs the question of whether the build-up of cheap renewable energy capacity can happen quickly enough for hydrogen to fulfil its potential. Ironically, a sizable part of the forecast extra demand for steel is destined for the construction of renewable power plants (Levi, 2021).

3 Silver-bullet solutions require increased precaution to prevent unintended consequences.

As often promised by new technologies, singular interventions with significant transformational potential can have critical unintended consequences. Today, India's Aadhaar digital identification (ID) system, introduced to ease welfare payments to India's most vulnerable and to combat fraud, includes 1.2 billion Indians (Dalberg, 2019). It allowed India to go from a digital backwater to being the world's largest market for digital real-time payments in less than a decade (ACI Worldwide, 2021). However, while it brought the majority of Indians into the system, it increased the gap with more than 100 million still marginalised Indians in harder-to-reach geographies or populations. Many private services like opening a bank account, getting access to food rationing or school admission, which are increasingly transitioning to Aadhaar too, are now even less accessible to those excluded. Furthermore, precautionary voices have warned of the tool's potential to facilitate a surveillance state (Amrute et al., 2020; Ritson, 2022).

Multiple researchers have suggested that microfinance is an effective intervention for the economic empowerment of the underprivileged, reducing poverty and vulnerability and building human capital (Swain, 2012; Arora et al., 2013). Lending to the unbanked, since Muhammad Yunus originally pioneered it in the 1980s, experienced exponential growth, reaching tens of millions of borrowers and winning him the Nobel Peace Prize in 2006. However, more recent studies have shown that microfinance not seldom leads to over-indebtedness and exploitation rather than empowerment (Schicks, 2013) and that the sector is especially vulnerable to economic shocks (Wagner & Winkler, 2013). Well-intended attempts to bring about systemic change require more deliberate upfront attention to identifying and mitigating unintended consequences.

4 WHY interventions require investment in collaborative processes.

Systemic change can take several decades and often involves interconnected changes to social practices, technologies, regulations, business models and societal norms. This inevitably involves conflicts over the direction and the pace of the change (Voulvoulis et al., 2022). The deeper leverage points have more significant transformational potential (Fischer & Riechers, 2018). However, it cannot be assumed that change in the WHY realm will not be met with resistance, especially when deeply held norms and values are questioned. It is essential to tackle this resistance and to provide new alternatives and opportunities (Pelling & Manuel-Navarrete, 2011). Without creating a constructive and trusted environment in which system partners feel secure enough to question the current dominant system and transcend its underlying paradigms; without investment in a deep, joint understanding of the system; without paying more attention to building and embedding the shared mindset and vision across the system's stakeholders, and without incentives for system-actors to collaborate for systemic change, progress is doomed to be limited.

A deep understanding by all stakeholders of the human or societal need underlying the system, the multiple actors and dynamics involved in satisfying this need and the life-cycle impacts that the current system is causing is crucial to inform the shared objectives in any collaborative effort for systemic change. Intra-company, intra-industry or technology-centric efforts to reduce impact offer at best partial solutions, often running the risk of not necessarily reducing but rather relocating life-cycle impact. For example, the car industry moving from combustible to electric motors does not automatically mean that the environmental impact is reduced. In fact, it relocates most of the life-cycle impact to electricity and battery production. Even though the life-cycle impact will come down as the world moves from fossil to renewable sources of energy, the embedded carbon footprint of an electric car today, because of the battery (depending on size and the energy source used in production), is significantly higher than that of a combustible engine vehicle. Moreover, it causes enormous other impacts, such as water depletion, toxic waste, human rights violations and others in the mining for components like cobalt and lithium, whose ominous nickname 'white oil' is already unleashing a gold rush of its own in geographies such as Chile and Bolivia (Balch, 2020). Because demand for batteries will lead to resource scarcity and the need for new mines, electric vehicles (EVs) might save car manufacturers but they won't save the planet.

5 Old mindsets are unlikely to produce a new system.

Risk management as a mindset will not bring us the change to sustainable models that the world needs. Some important risk factors, such as regulatory risk, materialise too late, as regulation typically is put in place (long) after the damage has been done. Instead, a risk management mindset incentivises greenwashing and lobbying to avoid disruption and maintain the status quo. For example, Exxon and other big oil players knew of the risks of climate change to society forty years before the world started to change policies, a move that many fossil fuel companies have overtly and covertly tried to delay, despite knowing the link between their business and climate change. Risk management is not a solution, especially if targets are set up as deals between industry sectors and governments, heavily influenced by industry lobbyists and biased towards the status quo. In the context of the Conference of Parties (COP) meetings, whose objective is to find a multilateral agreement to avoid climate change, it is particularly ironic that 636 fossil fuel lobbyists participated in the 2022 COP27 meeting yet that the 2023 COP28 meeting will be held in the United Arab Emirates (UAE) and chaired by the head of UAE oil giant Abu Dhabi National Oil Company (Singh Khadka, 2023).

As long as companies are knowingly causing environmental or social costs without paying for them, they are growing their profits unethically. The International Monetary Fund (n.d.) estimates that the implicit global subsidy to the fossil fuel industry from undercharging energy supply costs amounted to $531 billion in 2021. If also taking into account the cost borne by society for climate, environmental and air pollution impacts and foregone consumption taxes, the implicit subsidy was as much as $5.9 trillion ($11 million per minute), or 6.8 per cent of global GDP – expected to rise to 7.4 per cent of GDP in 2025 (Parry et al., 2021). In testimony before a US Congressional subcommittee in April 2021, teen activist Greta Thunberg spoke out about the hypocrisy of governments boasting of lofty goals while funding the very legacy sectors they say they want to phase out or transform: 'the fact that we are still having this discussion, and even more that we are still subsidising fossil fuels, directly or indirectly, using taxpayer money, is a disgrace' (Cornwell, 2021, p. 1).

Internalising the environmental and social costs into the cost calculation of companies would reflect an environmentally sustainable and intergenerationally just growth paradigm that incentivises companies to design better systems for all current and future stakeholders.

6 Big commitments need reinforcement.

There is no lack of ambition and commitment towards radical change to achieve sustainability goals. However, history has demonstrated a tendency for businesses and governments to make pledges that could not produce the expected outcomes. Many of these pledges set ambitious objectives but fail to change the system's deeper dynamics because they fall short of efforts to change the paradigm and the underlying mindset of the internal and external stakeholders involved. This results in poor incentives, shallow alignment and a lack of collaboration and support to achieve the goals.

The highest-profile pledge of the twenty-first century so far has emerged from the 2016 Paris climate agreement and the subsequent COP meetings. However, despite all national commitments, based on current plans, instead of the 45 per cent reduction compared to 2010 levels that will be required to stay within the 1.5°C of global warming agreed as a target, CO_2-eq emissions are still anticipated to rise by 10 per cent by 2030, and the IPCC moreover has highlighted severe delays in implementation of national plans.

According to Net Zero Tracker (2022), as of June 2022, more than 35 per cent of the top publicly traded corporations in the world committed to net zero, but 65 per cent still lack a detailed plan for how to get there. Only 38 per cent of the pledges include Scope 3 emissions, which comprise all indirect emissions throughout a company's value chain and typically account for between 65 per cent and 95 per cent of a product's life-cycle emissions (PwC, n.d.). Similarly, in 2018, more than 500 governments and businesses, representing 20 per cent of all plastic packaging produced globally, signed the New Plastics Economy Global Commitment, pledging to transition towards a circular economy for plastic (Ellen MacArthur Foundation, 2022). However, the 2022 report reveals that signatories have made little progress.

Without further systemic changes or regulatory reinforcement, many voluntary commitments risk lending themselves to greenwashing or changes in scope, targets or measurement criteria as time passes. Ironically, the resulting scrutiny of corporate commitments is leading to greenhushing, that is, corporate players being reluctant to publicly announce their environmental and societal impact targets and strategies. Reportedly, 25 per cent of corporate players are practising greenhushing (Speed, 2022).

Box 2 Rethinking Mobility

While collaborative efforts to reduce the impact of existing supply chains are laudable, we need to dedicate more effort and creativity to system reinvention. We can do this by asking ourselves how the same human or societal need can be met in ways other than the dominant legacy system. Systemic change does not start by aiming to optimise today's production assets; instead, a consumer-centric design-thinking approach, focussing on creatively solving the consumer or societal need at hand, can lead to drastically different solutions to current challenges, often uncovering additional systemic benefits. In this process, it is helpful to reflect on what paradigms are underlying the old and the new systems. For example, we need light, heat and cooling, but we do not necessarily need kilowatt-hours. Humans must consume proteins, but no law states that these must come from animal meat. We need health care, but is this best achieved by preventing or curing disease? Similarly, we need mobility, but do we necessarily need individual car ownership?

Questioning the need for individual car ownership or the need for moving around in the first place could help us creatively rethink mobility. For example, car-sharing schemes or cheaper taxis through driverless cars radically reduce the need for cars and parking space while still moving people comfortably around. Studies in the Netherlands and Germany showed that car sharing brought down CO_2 per kilometre driven by 8 to 16 per cent compared to private car ownership due to behaviour change and the need for fewer cars (PBL, 2015; Roth, 2022). At the same time, it is not unreasonable to wonder whether the wide availability of shared or not-owned cars might trigger a feedback loop that reduces the perception of car ownership as a status symbol.

Improving and stimulating public transport use would allow for a systemic impact. For example, experiments with heavily subsidised public transport in Germany and Spain in 2022 reduced air pollution and CO_2 emissions from car users switching to public transport while lowering inflation, even though the schemes overshot their objectives: high popularity of the plan in Germany, where 52 million monthly tickets were sold, also resulted in overcrowded trains and a high price tag for the government (Connolly, 2022). Similarly, stimulating bike use through bike sharing saves even more CO_2 and significantly impacts physical and mental health (Celis-Morales et al., 2017).

Systemic thinking about mobility and its impacts is also manifest in the design of mixed-use developments that provide space for work, living and leisure all within the same district, thus reducing the need for transport altogether. One example of this concept is the ambitious $3.9 billion One Bangkok project that is under development in Thailand; it is one of the largest of its kind in Southeast Asia.

These approaches, which structurally change the need for, and the mix of, modes of transport, have the potential not only to reduce CO_2 emissions and expenses and improve health but also to reduce the estimated 40 per cent of city centre space that is currently dedicated to roads and parking, freeing it up for much-needed housing, urban farming and public parks, all with their consequential benefits.

2.3 Complex Systemic Change in Practice: The EU's Farm to Fork Strategy

Established in the 1960s, Europe's Common Agricultural Policy (CAP), which occupies more than a third of the EU's budget, aimed to optimise cheap food production by subsidising large-scale farming across the continent. While this objective made sense in the early days, the CAP has become an indirect subsidy to support EU-based food companies' international competitiveness in their export markets.

Its focus on industrial, conventional farming practices had significant sustainability implications, driving biodiversity collapse in Europe, especially close to areas of intense livestock farming, and contributing to the global climate catastrophe, while eroding the food sovereignty of the destination markets of Europe's subsidised food, causing local farmers to be exploited or go out of business, while at the same time making European farmers overly dependent on the subsidies and taking up ever more of the EU budget (Abboud, 2018). For example, according to European Commission data, up to 90 per cent of cattle farmers' income is derived from subsidies, despite indications that as much as 87 per cent of global farming subsidies – approximately $470 billion – is distorting price and environmentally and socially harmful (FAO, 2021).

The Farm to Fork (F2F) strategy is Europe's effort to reinvent its old unsustainable food system (European Union, 2020). To evaluate the effectiveness of Europe's F2F strategy, we will apply the levers framework outlined in Section 2.1. By examining the F2F strategy through this lens, we can gain a comprehensive understanding of its potential impact and identify areas that may require further attention or enhancement to achieve the desired systems transformation.

2.3.1 WHAT: The Conditions of the System

While the measures in the CAP mainly revolved around, directly and indirectly, subsidising farming output and supply chain inputs to make European farming more cost-competitive, current reform proposals, while not wholly abolishing farmer subsidies, call for a mandatory cap on per-farm subsidies to reduce the benefits accumulating with large landowners. In addition to this, farmer income support will become conditional on farmers adhering to the environment- and climate-friendly farming practices and standards, called the Good Agricultural and Ecological Conditions (GAEC); farmers will be prioritised according to whether or not they perform additional activities that are related to climate, the environment, animal welfare and antimicrobial resistance and whether or not they contribute to reaching the targets of the EU Green Deal. The extent to which CAP measures (read: subsidies) can be aligned with the new F2F strategy will be critical. The F2F strategy is furthermore considering value-added tax (VAT) reform to allow member states to send the right signals to consumers by, for example, lowering VAT on healthy and sustainable food, such as fruits and vegetables, and encouraging a shift from animal products to a more plant-based diet. The strategy's potential for bringing about a genuine change in the EU food systems will to a significant extent depend on the ability of the EU's leadership to resolve stakeholder resistance and continue political momentum, which has stalled due to the challenging economic environment post-Covid and the impacts of the war in Ukraine (Schebesta & Candel, 2020).

In comparison, in Southeast Asia, the ASEAN Integrated Food Security (AIFS) framework and strategic plan of action, developed by the Association of Southeast Asian Nations (ASEAN), aim to ensure long-term food security and improve the livelihoods of farmers in the region by facilitating systemic change through cross-sectoral collaboration among member states and a comprehensive approach that considers the interrelated factors of food production, distribution, access and utilisation (Association of Southeast Asian Nations, 2020). However, most interventions are mainly situated in the low-potential WHAT realm. For example, in the distribution aspect, ASEAN nations mitigate market impacts through market controls and economic measures like export restrictions, price controls, subsidies and selected import facilitation. Successful implementation of this framework may be hindered by several challenges, for example a lack of cooperation and legal obligation between member states (Islam & Kieu, 2020), which might be an indication of the limited attention given to levers in the HOW and WHY realms.

2.3.2 HOW: The Dynamics of the System

The European Commission explicitly included provisions on governance and collective involvement of stakeholders in a legislative framework for sustainable food systems. It actively encouraged multi-stakeholder dialogue with farmers, the food industry, civil society and academia in designing policies for the new food system. This, for example, resulted in the multi-stakeholder-informed EU Code of Conduct on responsible marketing and business practices.

Despite this, criticism has been raised that the F2F strategy was not supported by an impact assessment, and there are some indications that shaping the F2F strategy might have suffered from a (perceived) lack of ability by the stakeholders to influence the structure and rules of the new system (Wesseler, 2022). Moreover, as F2F objectives divert from the current CAP focus on subsidising farmers and companies, aligning CAP with the F2F strategy has not been without resistance (Corporate Europe Observatory, 2020). Farmer unions, fearing that F2F will increase costs and reduce competitiveness, have held intense protests, like the ones that paralysed the Netherlands in 2022 and triggered solidarity protests by farmers in other parts of Europe, and intensified lobbying efforts by farmer unions and industries like the pesticide industry. Taking advantage of the Russian invasion of Ukraine, these industrial farming lobbies claim that food security is at risk in the European Union and are calling on the European Commission to set aside sustainable agriculture objectives for the moment (Corporate Europe Observatory, 2022).

To enhance information flows and collective learning, through the EU's Horizon Europe fund (2021–7) and the European Innovation Partnership (EIP Agri) and other vehicles, the F2F strategy made €10 billion available to facilitate collaboration between researchers, industry and other stakeholders for research and innovation related to food, bioeconomy, natural resources, agriculture, fisheries, aquaculture and the environment.

Already, the CAP and F2F feature feedback loops through the EU Emissions Trading System (ETS) and agriculture subsidies for reducing GHG emissions. In addition, information flows to farmers will be enhanced through a Farm Sustainability Data Network, with data and advice on sustainable farming practices, further supported by proposals for more stringent regulations on feed additives, food waste and animal welfare. An essential additional lever aiming to strengthen positive feedback loops under the F2F strategy is to improve information flows towards the public. This includes yet-contested proposals for a harmonised food labelling framework that covers mandatory front-of-pack nutritional data and climate, environmental and social aspects of food products. Besides this, the European Commission supports small and medium-sized enterprises (SMEs) and invests in education and engagement of consumers to raise awareness and mobilise action to accelerate the transition.

2.3.3 WHY: The Purpose of the System

The old CAP was based on the paradigms that cheap food is the best way to feed a growing world population and that, therefore, a cost-competitive agricultural sector is good for Europe. The unintended negative consequences of that policy have forced Europe to question those paradigms. The F2F strategy is based on the belief that healthy food produced in environmentally sustainable, affordable and socially just ways will reduce the current system's inefficiencies. The emerging paradigm, therefore, is that our food system should work with nature, not against it, and that no one should be left behind.

While the CAP's main objective was to produce cheap food, the comprehensive EU Biodiversity and F2F strategies, based on these new paradigms, aim to transform our food system into a more sustainable and equitable model. Specific F2F targets include a 50 per cent reduction in pesticide and antimicrobials, a 50 per cent per capita food waste reduction, a 20 per cent reduction in fertiliser use, and having 25 per cent of EU farmland under organic production by 2030.

Not all aspects of systemic change can be fully controlled, but deliberate systemic change needs a collaborative, holistic approach with a leverage points perspective, recognising the influential WHAT, HOW and WHY interventions in the system. Nevertheless, as the efforts to reform the food system show, collaboration is complex. In 2012, a global C-suite study (IBM, 2012) of 1,709 chief executive officers (CEOs) found that 75 per cent saw collaboration as the key to future success. Yet multiple analysts have concluded that most collaborations fail to deliver sustained supernormal value (Fawcett et al., 2015). So how can we create the conditions that improve stakeholder collaboration to achieve the systemic changes we need?

3 Creating the Conditions for Collaborative Systemic Change

There are limitations to what can be done in isolation. Multi-stakeholder collaboration is pertinent in achieving systemic change. Literature on sustainable pathways emphasises that sustainability issues involve dynamics, complexity, uncertainty and competing interests (Leach et al., 2010). Based on their systematised review of literature on cross-sector partnerships and systemic change, Clarke & Crane (2018) underline the interdisciplinary nature of systemic change and the crucial role of interaction between system-actors and subsystems. They suggest that it is a type of change that is conceptually underdeveloped. Kingston and Caballero (2009), when analysing institutional change, describe two different schools of interpretation of change: one being the deliberate creation of institutions through a political process and the other emphasising the spontaneous emergence of new institutions through evolutionary processes. Research on innovation systems has influenced our understanding of this decentralised process of 'emergence' or 'incrementalism', the way large-scale, systemic transformation can emerge from multiple small and incremental changes that result from co-evolutionary interactions between various human systems, such as values, knowledge, organisation and technology, and environment systems at different scale-levels (Freeman, 1991; Norgaard 1995, 2006; Malerba, 2002). Illustrating this theory of the multi-level dynamic of socio-technical transitions, Geels (2005) describes how the transition from horse-carriages to trams to automobiles happened through a confluence and interaction of evolutions at multiple levels and in multiple domains, including health and safety concerns, cost considerations, population growth, suburbanisation, technological innovation, economic independence, user preferences and policy decisions.

Emergence, or incrementalism, may not be able to address the urgency, complexity and interconnected nature of systemic problems. It risks creating specific interventions focussing on individual components or aspects of a system and staying limited to incremental changes from the status quo rather than the radical changes required at the systems level. Moreover, it is argued that careful plotting of a series of small incremental victories to achieve a significant change is impossible because conditions do not remain constant (Weick, 1984). However, transitions scholars have investigated the governance of transitions in socio-technical systems (Smith & Stirling, 2005; Foxon et al., 2009; Loorbach, 2010), presuming that although change cannot be controlled, it can be guided through goal-oriented modulation of co-evolutionary change processes (Kemp et al., 2007). This is consistent with the belief that systemic change emerges from the interaction of top-down institutional conditions and bottom-up (catalytic and disruptive) innovation, facilitated by institutional entrepreneurs and networks at numerous organisational levels (Westley et al., 2011), and with Grunwald's (2007) concept of directed incrementalism, which seeks to connect long-term sustainability goals with the realities of incremental decisions made in the present. Kingston and Caballero (2009) and Reimers and Li (2012) argue for integrating elements of evolution and deliberate design into a broader theory of institutional change.

Because systems are made up of multiple actors and interrelated factors, each with their own subsystems, contexts and dynamics, solving complex systemic issues requires multiple actors to collaborate (Bryson et al., 2006, 2015). Collaboration in the context of systemic change could be defined as collaboration between partners from at least two different sectors seeking to achieve sustainable value creation at a systemic level, However, multi-stakeholder cross-sector collaboration comes with numerous challenges with respect to design, governance and implementation (Vangen et al., 2015). In the context of system change, one such challenge could be identifying the collaborative advantage: 'collaborators must make sure there is a clear collaborative advantage to be gained by collaborating, meaning that collaborators can gain something significant together that they could not achieve alone' (Bryson et al., 2015, p. 647). The systems thinking required to identify these advantages is essential for change but can also be uncomfortable and messy (Senge et al., 2007). As a conceptual tool, systems thinking can help identify these advantages, but at the same time it could allow for different and conflicting views within the multi-stakeholder collaboration as the stakeholders involved could have different worldviews that inform the notion of sustainability. It is therefore essential to develop a shared conceptual 'systems sense' that includes the ruling norms and paradigms.

In addition, establishing the right partner connections is necessary to create a basis for systemic change within a specific system. According to Mishra et al. (2019), this is especially necessary in developing countries, where most of the world's population resides. They argue that collaboration failures in a supply chain mainly occur in developing countries as they encounter more constraints due to various reasons, including resource management problems, limited economic capacity, inadequate training, a lack of advanced technology, inaccurate available information, low resource taxes and even no political support and weak demand for environmentally superior technologies. Multi-stakeholder collaboration is pertinent to overcoming these barriers as good working relationships can help foster a shared understanding of the challenges, accelerate the adoption of sustainable practices, provide incentives and adapt education to local needs to eventually create effective partnerships and a basis for systemic change (Jia et al., 2018).

In collaboration, we need to avoid a status of 'deep incumbency', for example where the interests of specific firms or lobby groups become so entangled with those of the government that it becomes difficult to conceptualise a functional regime in the absence of those firms or groups (Johnstone et al., 2017). Therefore, efforts to shape pathways towards a sustainable society require addressing contested values, multiple narratives of change and the politics of knowledge, as well as questioning dominant paradigms, empowering margin-alised stakeholders and putting businesses, institutions and politics centre stage (Stirling, 2014; Scoones et al., 2015).

System-level thinking encourages and enables constructive dialogue and collaborative action across businesses, governments, financial markets and civil society, transcending self-interested lobbying and defensive reactions that hamper systemic change efforts today, as seen in some of the examples described in previous sections. In collaborating, these systemic actors will not only enrich each other's understanding of the complex bigger system but together they can create the perfect storm of policy incentives, co-innovation systems and financial returns that will encourage companies to disrupt legacy models and build future-fit growth models.

To enable collaboration to shape holistic system interventions, the right condi-tions need to be created for critical stakeholder groups to collaborate. Based on the empirical research, the success of multi-stakeholder collaboration – and the identification of the collaborative advantage and a shared systems sense – depends on leadership aligning conditions, structures, processes and outcomes so that value can be created for all involved (Senge et al., 2007; Bryson et al., 2015). In their literature review of 301 articles on the food system (129 papers) and the energy system (172 papers), Dorninger et al. (2020) found that only 5 per cent of the reviewed papers studied interventions on the system's intent (the WHY) and that the deep systemic outcomes were limited, with 5 per cent creating a shift in norms and paradigms and only 6 per cent of the interventions leading to more system-level collaboration.

Given the importance of collaboration and the systemic change potential of WHY-level interventions, in this section we will first explore the conditions that are conducive to multi-stakeholder collaboration for systems change, before more specifically looking at how the conditions can be created to optimise two powerful levers that have remained relatively underexposed in previous research:

1. enhancing business-led collaboration for systemic change
2. equipping stakeholders with future-fit mindsets from which the design of our new systems will emerge.

3.1 Conditioning Factors for Systemic Interventions

In practice, multi-stakeholder collaborations are challenging for all parties involved, and this often leads to suboptimal outcomes. Systemic change is

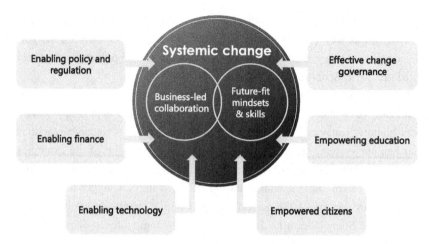

Figure 5 Conditioning factors for systemic interventions.

complex and contested, and its co-evolving nature raises significant questions regarding what factors can move system-actors to collectively seek systemic change. Different actors and factors can influence and create the conditions to enhance the systemic impact of these levers (see Figure 5).

3.1.1 Enabling Policy and Regulation

While China and the USA are using the public sector's financial muscle to pick industry winners and shape systems, the European Parliament decided to drive systemic change by using the €95.5 billion Horizon Europe research and innovation programme to orient industrial strategy towards five concrete missions, including climate change adaptation, smart cities and restoration of water bodies and soils (European Commission, 2021). Policymakers can greatly encourage corporate system-actors to drive systemic change by providing clarity and consistency of policy support, objectives and indicators. In return, businesses can act as advocates and implementation partners for progressive public policy.

Regulations like Extended Producer Responsibility (EPR) effectively encourage corporate players to take responsibility for their system-level impact and align wider system partners for system reinvention and impact. Progressive policy and regulation could even be initiated by industry itself. Since 2012, the producer organisations of the Dutch textile and fashion industry have been actively making joint efforts to achieve structural sustainability improvements in their sector. They initiated a voluntary EPR scheme, in collaboration with the government, that makes textile and garment producers collectively responsible for the reuse, recycling and reprocessing of used clothes and textiles, as part of the transition to a circular economy by 2050 and the halving of primary raw material use by 2030 (Hanemaaijer et al., 2021). Producers and importers on the Dutch market will pay a fee per product, contributing to an innovation fund to stimulate circular and sustainable business models and initiatives within their sector.

Not only corporate and civil society input into the design of future-fit policies but also e-governance and societal participation in the enforcement of impact-oriented regulation can help cement and anchor the mindsets required for the transition towards more sustainable future growth models (Hellström, 2009). Although the setting of indicators and objectives seems like a successful lever to drive change, such efforts should be mindful of Goodhart's Law, which describes how a measure can lose its value for good when it becomes an indicator or policy target. In other words, what you end up measuring is not always a genuine and direct representation of what you set out to influence (Strathern, 1997). Instead, the indicator affects all the actions, compliance and assessments involved in realising that target, causing it to lose its informational value and undermining the goal (Kim, 2023). For example, to measure a country's economic health, only the GDP growth rate is used as an indicator. This can lead to boosting GDP as the primary focus instead of considering the economic well-being of all economic actors.

3.1.2 Enabling Finance

Innovative finance has helped accelerate many of society's significant transformations, from fuelling the growth of colonisation and international trade in the seventeenth century to greasing the wheels of the Industrial Revolution in the nineteenth (Heaton, 1937). But capitalism has often been criticised for focussing too much on short-term interests and financial returns and failing to correctly internalise the multiple external costs it causes (Scitovsky, 1954; De Grauwe, 2017). Financial institutions are now in a privileged position to become an authentic catalyst for the biggest transformation of our century. However, this systemic transformation towards more sustainable models will require purposeful, in some cases blended, finance with a longer-term horizon, and investment decisions that consider social and environmental costs and objectives in addition to financial returns. Further, the environmental, social and governance (ESG) ratings currently being championed by the financial sector still have infant-stage drawbacks (Tricks, 2022). Addressing these challenges through international taxonomy, simplification and possibly disintegration of data to improve

transparency will restore trust and increase capital flow to sustainable investments; it will also anchor a sustainability mindset across business and finance
sectors.

3.1.3 Enabling Technology

Undoubtedly, both the emergence and the rapid development of information and
communication technology have brought about systemic change. More people are
connected to more information than ever before. As the regimes toppled during the
Arab spring can attest, citizens leveraging digital technologies can complicate the
relationship between governments and citizens. The Cambridge Analytica scandal
also showed how digital platforms can be used to manipulate public sentiment in
less noble ways. But technology can be leveraged to deliberately accelerate
systemic change. Progressive governments and businesses are discovering how
digital and mobile technology can be used constructively to provide new platforms
and tools to foster stakeholder dialogue and education, raise awareness, change
paradigms and build/strengthen mindsets and behaviours. The increased transparency and accountability, as well as the secure, smart contracts capability of
technologies such as blockchain in the food system, can change behaviour towards
more sustainable and healthy food choices (Lazaroiu et al., 2019) and reduce waste
and inefficiencies in supply chains (Nandi et al., 2021).

3.1.4 Empowered Citizens

Tackling the multiple global challenges that, by definition, involve everyone is
impossible without creating space for diverse voices and solutions. In
a democratic, dynamic and diverse society, implementing solutions to problems
depends heavily on the support of informed, critical thinking and active citizens
(Angheloiu & Tennant, 2020). Improving how we structure and organise our
information flows to and from relevant stakeholders allows participatory
approaches such as policy co-design or participatory budgeting to leverage
systemic change. In addition, we can evolve participation from being consultation
only to involving joint visioning processes to gather input from, for example,
marginalised groups, thus aiding the kind of more-inclusive and empowering
decision-making processes that are essential in any sustainability transition.

3.1.5 Empowering Education

Educational and leadership development organisations play a pivotal role in embedding the mindset, supporting the systemic understanding and developing the transformational skills of decision-makers and change agents across stakeholder groups

in our systems. Due to societal support being a critical aspect for the shaping and implementation of systemic change, the role of civil society and community organisations in building capacity and mindsets and facilitating collaboration among stakeholders should not be underestimated. Free education from online platforms like non-profit Khan Academy and Coursera, each with well over 100 million learners, is democratising education and could play an important role in helping to change perceptions and build systemic understanding and collaboration skills.

3.1.6 Effective Change Governance

How can governance facilitate or contribute to shaping or steering systemic transformations? It is tempting to focus only on the hard aspects of planning and managing a collaborative change process. However, critical and often underestimated are the soft factors of collaboration, the interaction that is needed between system partners in order for them to build trusted and constructive collaboration. Investment in these soft factors improves the effectiveness of the hard factors, which are strong foundations, alignment, momentum and inclusive leadership (see Figure 6 and Box 3). New hybrid forms of governance, such as multi-level governance, adaptive management and decentralisation, have become prevalent. Although these terms are conceptualised differently in practice, they share core principles: adaptive learning, self-organisation and diversity in cultures, institutions and processes (Vakkuri & Johanson, 2021).

3.2 Business-Led Collaboration for Systemic Change

Complex societal issues, such as the climate crisis, inequality, systemic racism and the degradation of natural capital, cannot be ignored by businesses anymore.

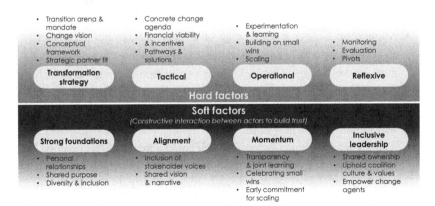

Figure 6 Hard and soft success factors of the collaborative transformation process.

Box 3 Managing Collaborative Transformation Efforts

Contemporary studies of transition management focus on the complex adaptive systems nature of transitions (Barton et al., 2018). According to Loorbach (2010), transition pathways generally identify four areas of activity:

- **Strategic**: Create a transition arena, particularly focussing on frontrunners and collaborative visioning.
- **Tactical**: Develop a concrete transition agenda, including possible transition paths and barriers to overcome.
- **Operational**: Encourage transition experiments and attempts to scale up promising options.
- **Reflexive**: Monitor, evaluate and reflect on actors, actions and progress towards the transition.

The importance of the relational aspect of these collaborative efforts, in addition to the conceptual and action-driven aspects of systemic change, was recognised by Senge et al. (2007). A 2016 study of thirty-nine complex cross-sectoral collaborations by Xynteo, GLTE and Royal Dutch Shell (2016) highlights the soft factors that are critical for successful collaborations and shared practical recommendations. Investment in these soft factors improves the effectiveness of the hard factors (see Figure 6), which are:

- **Strong foundations**: Partners should have a strategic fit and invest in building personal relationships. When co-developing a clear shared purpose, to clarify the reasons behind the partnership and the mutual necessity, it is imperative to ensure that the partnership is diverse and includes quieter, potentially influential voices.
- **Alignment**: Engage a wide range of stakeholders, gathering, sharing and evaluating data to come to a shared understanding of the context of the system challenge. This builds trust among partners, helps to identify potential conflicts and supports change efforts. Convert the shared vision into a short, engaging narrative; focussing at this stage on the why rather than the how or the what will help to keep the collaboration on track later. Appointing a neutral anchor can facilitate this process.
- **Momentum**: Maintain a collaborative mindset and ensure that new personnel joining the project understand the work's collaborative nature and shared objective. Encouraging mutuality and joint learning from pilot results and communicating quick wins builds trust internally and externally for scaling. Agreeing on early in-principle commitments for

scaling will allow the collaboration to keep the momentum into the scaling phase.

- **Inclusive leadership**: Identify where in the system the energy is to initiate change and empower change agents to drive the process. Foster a shared feeling of ownership and responsibility for change and ensure that the collaboration's own culture and the project's values come from enough different voices to be upheld by everyone.

This is true not only because these issues are materially affecting business and posing operational and compliance risks (Rogers, 2019) but also because policymakers and regulators are driving change, and increasingly discerning consumers expect businesses and industries to have a positive impact on natural and social capital (Mohr et al., 2005). Never before has the perfect storm been so promising – policymakers, business actors, finance, talent and consumers all desire change towards more sustainable approaches.

Businesses must play a leading role in solving many of the environmental and social challenges we face because governments do not have the expertise or permanence to do the work alone. Governments are limited by their borders and cannot attack systemic problems that are global in nature. Besides, they are limited by election cycles (Senge et al., 2007). Governments need the skills and knowledge of businesses to develop the transition's technical specificities and to institutionalise the transition mechanisms. Businesses have the reach, agility and intellectual and innovative capacity to be powerful drivers of the sustainability transition (Scheyvens et al., 2016). Risk sharing through blended public and private finance also facilitates the transformation to sustainable models (Choi & Seiger, 2020).

According to the Edelman Trust Barometer, in today's climate of economic and existential anxiety, polarisation and disinformation, business is the sole institution trusted by the public as competent and ethical compared with non-governmental organisations (NGOs), government and media (Edelman Trust Institute, 2023). As a result, business is under pressure to step into the void left by government. The public expects businesses to lead on societal issues, driving collaboration with government, restoring economic optimism and advocating for the truth. This would increase levels of trust and support for measures proposed by both governmental and business leaders while accelerating the sustainability transition the world needs.

Societal stakeholders have compelling reasons to collaborate. Business is inherently motivated to organise resources to respond to needs and capture commercial opportunities in suboptimal systems. Governments are focussed on shaping systems that support societies' needs as effectively as possible. And in free societies it is only when business and government effectively satisfy societies' needs that citizens are willing to extend them their licence to operate and govern.

As described earlier, collaborative systemic change is often a complex co-evolutionary process involving multiple actors and subsystems; however, it can be initiated and driven by a dominant actor with a strategic agency. Government-initiated institutional or systemic change is often associated with top-down, centrally planned change efforts. For example, one could think of the rigorous city development and digital transformation efforts driven by the Singaporean government (Tan, 2020). This could also take the form of a powerful multinational driving implementation of a transformational new policy in its supply chain. Even though this section focusses on business-led collaboration for systemic change, the concept of strategic-agency-driven systemic change begs the controversial question of to what extent authoritarian regimes are better positioned to address systemic issues. Gilley (2012) suggests that authoritarian regimes may effectively produce policy outputs related to sustainability challenges, but the impact on policy outcomes is unclear. Several authors have suggested that systemic change is more likely to occur in authoritarian regimes when there is social pressure for change and when the government is able to make policy concessions or during times of crisis (Chan, 2013; Chen & Xu, 2017).

In the same vein, the complex and multi-stakeholder nature of many of our big challenges would lead one to expect that societies with a collectivist mindset could be better set up to collaborate to face systemic issues than individualistic societies. Dutch social psychologist Geert Hofstede (2011) observed there to be a radical difference between the extreme individualism prevalent in the USA and Europe and the collectivist cultures of East and Southeast Asia. The relatively harmonious public response to the initial Covid-19 outbreak in East and Southeast Asia compared to Europe and the USA seems to illustrate this. Measures to curb public behaviour in East and Southeast Asia did not meet with public resistance. They managed to limit the spread of Covid-19 relatively successfully. At the same time, EU and US outbreaks got out of control in large part because of a strong reluctance of the individuals in those locations to adopt a common behaviour. The EU and the USA survived more by the grace of the virus mutating into a less deadly variant than because they managed to contain the spread through behaviour change. At the root of this collectivist behaviour is the paradigm that societies develop more harmoniously when people display civil behaviour in the interest of the whole rather than individualistic behaviour guided by self-interest.

Systemic change efforts can also be initiated by a corporate actor or coalition of actors mobilising entire supply chains to take innovative approaches to old problems. An example of such a business-driven and regulator-supported transformation of critical systems is when telecommunications company Vodafone in 2007 launched a mobile money-transfer system, M-PESA, in Kenya (McKinsey & Company, 2022). By leveraging the country's high mobile-phone penetration rate, M-PESA offered a new service to the unbanked members of Kenya's population, who previously had to rely on inefficient and insecure cash-based payments. Financial institutions, regulators and the Central Bank of Kenya worked together to support regulation. Today, nearly 50 per cent of the country's GDP flows through M-PESA, and 2 per cent of Kenyan households have been lifted from poverty. At the same time, more than 51 million customers use M-PESA across seven African nations.

Visionary corporate players and progressive supply chain partners that take leadership positions in the reinvention of the systems they operate in will reap unprecedented benefits. Empirical evidence over recent years has shown that purpose-driven companies at the forefront of the sustainability transition attract highly motivated employees and see higher sales growth from increased customer loyalty and higher levels of innovation; they also improve operational risk and supply chain resilience, and see this reflected in higher valuations and lower cost of capital (Freiberg et al., 2020).

But how can companies develop into transformational organisations, and become drivers of systemic change? Let's first explore what makes transformational organisations different.

3.2.1 Transformational Organisations

Making the world into a better, more sustainable place requires more than a smart marketing campaign, ticking a few ESG boxes or installing EV charging poles. To transform our value-creation models into models that build economic but also natural and social capital, we need leaders and companies that go beyond lip service and greenwashing. It requires companies that feel responsible not only for their operations but also for the value and impacts to society that they create through the wider systems in which they participate. These transformational organisations have social responsibility and sustainable thinking ingrained in their culture and day-to-day decision-making at all levels.

Corporate social responsibility (CSR) has evolved constantly in the last decades (Moura-Leite & Padgett, 2011). Carroll (2016) defines the economic, legal, ethical and philanthropic dimensions of CSR behaviour in his much-quoted CSR pyramid. Maon et al. (2010) offer a multidimensional, dynamic perspective of the CSR development process, based on a stakeholder-oriented conceptualisation of CSR that integrates moral, cultural and strategic aspects, together with its organisational implications. Even though the combination of political, economic,

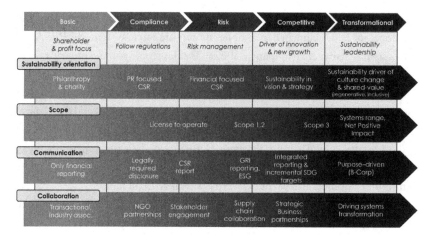

Figure 7 Evolution of corporate sustainability strategy.

social, environmental and regulatory trends may vary by region, from our experience assisting companies across multiple sectors in their sustainability journeys, a pattern emerges regarding how corporates' responsibility towards society tends to evolve in practice; this is true for most companies, from the most inward-looking to those that are increasingly outward-looking and transformational. Understanding this evolution will help companies recognise where in the evolution they are and how to evolve more quickly. Five stages of evolution can be identified (see Figure 7), each with distinct characteristics in terms of the motivation and scope of the organisation's socially responsible behaviour, how it engages stakeholders and how it communicates its contribution to a more sustainable world (Van der Zanden, 2022):

1 Basic Phase

In the period before the social and environmental costs caused by business were recognised as compromising our longer-term ability to create corporate and societal value, most businesses had a different predominant focus. As Milton Friedman (1970) phrased it, 'the social responsibility of business is to increase its profits' (p.1). Externalities, the social and environmental costs of doing business, were typically not considered the responsibility of the company unless they directly affected the company's capacity to operate. Companies concentrated on maximising shareholder value, frequently in the near term, as capital markets evolved towards expecting quarterly financial reporting. Relationships with stakeholders like suppliers, employees and local communities were largely transactional; companies would draft in industry associations to lobby for their interests. If profits allowed, some owners of companies would donate to philanthropic or charitable causes to enhance their reputation and preserve their social licence to operate. Some companies still behave according to these basic principles.

2 Compliance Orientation

Stricter health, safety and environmental regulations reflected an increasing societal awareness of the need to protect workers, communities and the health of our planet. As fines, sometimes retroactive, could be severe, companies became concerned about abiding by the rules and 'doing no harm'. During this compliance-oriented phase, CSR often moved from the HSQE (health, safety, quality and environment) office, where it tended to originate, into the public affairs or communications space, as companies expanded their legal and communications departments. In this phase, CSR activities and partnerships with NGOs were frequently oriented towards showing the company to be a decent member of society, while restricting disclosure of environmental and social impacts to the legal minimum.

3 Risk Orientation

Environmental and social factors increasingly constituted legal and reputational risks to businesses. This was in addition to operational risks, like supply chain disruptions, which could also have a significant material impact. Often guided by the head of finance, companies in this stage of the CSR evolution handled these risks by adopting a more structured approach towards evaluating the material risks to their business. They introduced ESG rating as a framework through which to quantify the level of risk embedded in their sustainability performance, although this not infrequently led to some form of greenwashing. They also began to publish CSR reports, disclosing the risks and impacts via materiality analysis. They primarily used stakeholder engagement to monitor and manage potential conflicts.

4 Competitive Awakening

As businesses began to understand that tackling sustainability challenges could result in better resource management, increased resilience, lower cost of capital, stronger innovation and new market opportunities, sustainability began to take on a more strategic role. This is where the chief sustainability officer – one of the fastest-growing new roles in recent years, according to a PwC study (PwC, 2022b) – entered the picture, and frequently the board room. To fully capitalise on this competitive potential, companies in this phase attempted to articulate a vision for sustainability as a new growth opportunity and to engage in programmes to integrate sustainability throughout the functional areas and levels of the company. This was frequently done in conjunction with voluntary disclosure of impacts and mitigation measures on a broader range of sustainability issues, as well as setting and reporting progress on specific and incremental SDG targets. Because, typically, the majority of life-cycle impact occurs in the upstream and downstream supply chain (Scope 3), companies engaged their supply chain partners, exploring opportunities to collaboratively find solutions with positive impact and/or commercial promise.

5 Transformational Organisations

Nowadays, an increasing number of enlightened leaders are championing sustainability because it is the right thing to do in order to build a better, more sustainable society. They recognise that business cannot prosper in the long run if it is at the expense of natural and social, or human, capital. These leaders demonstrate vision and purpose; they feel responsible not only for their organisations but also for the larger system in which they operate. Rather than lobbying for industry interests, transformational organisations advocate cross-sector collaboration and rally stakeholders across the supply chain and industries into joining forces for the sustainable reinvention and transformation of the systems they are a part of, whether the food system, the energy system or the health system. In addition, transformational businesses act as advocates for progressive, holistic public policy, as both hard policies, such as laws and regulations, and soft policies, such as subsidies and tax incentives, impact the performance of a system. This advocacy, at the same time as businesses demonstrate that market demand exists for sustainable solutions and pro-climate reforms, will give policymakers the confidence to support systemic change. We can see this already happening in the food system, where investments in bovine food additives and other methods for lowering emissions from livestock are being developed by several corporate players. At the same time, governments around the world are subsidising $360 million in research into alternative, sustainable proteins, including cultivated meat and fermentation-based foods (Good Food Institute, 2022).

Companies that demonstrate transformational leadership in addressing complex societal issues, like plastic waste, inequality, migration and water scarcity, are deliberately pursuing the creation of shared value, exploring regenerative and inclusive growth models. A crucial function of the chief sustainability officer is to be a catalyst of cultural change, building a transformative movement rooted in a sustainable mindset and collaborative behaviour across all company levels (Greenwald, 2023).

BOX 4 TRANSFORMATIONAL POTENTIAL OF FINANCE

Because of the enabling role of finance, the banking sector has great potential as a driver of systemic transformation. As of 2021, nearly 5,000 financial institutions managing more than $120 trillion in assets had signed up to the United Nations Principles of Responsible Investment (2022), committing to incorporate ESG considerations in their investment decisions. The ESG rating concept championed by the sector to enable investors to optimise social and environmental impacts alongside financial returns could establish a powerful feedback loop influencing investor decisions. Critics, however, say that ESG rating was invented by the sector rather to create a new service offering (read: revenue opportunity) and investment category, a way for some banks to gain credibility in their efforts to capture ESG funds (Tricks, 2022).

After an initial gold rush into ESG funds in the decade up to 2021 and ESG funds outperforming non-ESG returns, the infant-stage drawbacks of ESG rating (complexity, cost and quality of data, lack of transparency, inconsistency across rating agencies, ambiguous weighting of different categories, risk of greenwashing) generated controversy and even political backlash in the USA (Temple-West & Masters, 2023). Addressing the ESG rating challenges is essential to restore trust in ESG investing, return capital inflows and further anchor a sustainability mindset across business and finance sectors. An international taxonomy, simplification – perhaps focussing mainly on the 'E' – and possibly disintegrating the rating to improve the transparency of ESG data and the weighting in the rating process could all contribute to this.

Impact-oriented funding could facilitate projects that aim to improve system-level impacts. The private impact market grew to approximately $1.2 trillion at the end of 2021 – up 63 per cent since 2019, according to the Global Impact Investing Network, an international think tank on impact investing – but it is still a small part of the total assets under management (Hand et al., 2022). The European Commission has made €20 billion available through the Just Transition Mechanism to support companies and regions through the transition to carbon neutrality. In addition, to increase transformation funding, the EU Invest Fund and the European Investment Bank (EIB) are allowing highly regulated banks to offer riskier sustainability credits by offering sustainability guarantees covering 70 per cent of bank investments.

Scandinavian Nordea Bank is one of the pioneering banks that are proactively driving system transformation by taking on activist shareholder roles and growing their sustainability advisory offering to help their corporate customers develop transition plans or simplify ESG reporting for SMEs. The bank also mobilises innovation partners to develop new sustainable products, such as financing for circular business models.

3.2.2 How to Become a Transformational Organisation

Most people and companies want to be good citizens and contribute to a better world. But how do you mobilise an organisation's resources and capabilities so that the organisation can purposefully evolve towards being transformational, creating value by driving change towards sustainable models of growth within itself, its supply chain and the larger system it operates in?

A guideline for transforming organisations, provided by Serfontein et al. (2009), describes factors such as strategy, organisational design, organisational culture, leadership and communication. Karp (2006) highlights the role of leadership during transformations and, given the chaotic nature of change processes, advocates for taking a systemic view and applying principles of self-organising to foster a facilitative environment when transforming organisations. In practice, harnessing the power of business to build a more inclusive, equitable and regenerative global economy, movements like B Corp are encouraging a growing group of certified corporate members to become champions of systemic transformation and promoting a systemic mindset through adherence to the B Corp standards.

While cultural and strategic contexts can vary, we have extracted a framework based on three essential pillars from our observation of the evolution of organisations with ambitions to demonstrate sustainability leadership and systemic agency. Companies that evolve successfully into transformational organisations ensure that they invest in developing strategic clarity, shaping their organisational behaviour and building the required ecosystems for innovation and scaling of impact. Within these three building blocks, further concrete steps can be identified (see Figure 8).

1 Strategy and Foresight

The most successful transformational companies dedicate resources to open-mindedly and proactively exploring strategic scenarios and evaluating how to prepare the company to move into new markets and realities. This can take the form of disruption teams, which are tasked with monitoring potentially disruptive forces, such as technological developments, supply- and demand-side disruptions or institutional change, and reinventing the company, that is, self-disrupting before being disrupted, which D'Aveni (1999) describes as a sign of strategic

Figure 8 Roadmap towards becoming a transformational organisation.

supremacy. To avoid the limitations of incumbent mindsets, these disruption teams often include external agitators and report directly to C-level to protect them from the immune system of the core business.

2 New Growth Narrative

Scholars have underlined the powerful role of narratives in change processes (Sonenshein, 2010; Vaara et al., 2016). Narratives mobilise change most effectively if they communicate the purpose and the strategic imperative for change through the value frame of the stakeholders (Parmar et al., 2010). Building on strategic foresight, transformational leaders develop and anchor new narratives that inspire internal change and enable external market position. They describe a vision and objectives, inspiring and empowering the organisation to develop concrete measures to achieve these.

3 Leadership and Learning

In many cases, developing a company into a transformational sustainability leader requires updating the competencies of its key personnel, especially their communication and joint visioning skills, so that they can excel as change leaders through the transition process (Doyle, 2002; Vakola et al., 2007). Getting a critical mass of people in the organisation to operate with the right mindset and skills can be achieved through talent acquisition, 'hiring into the new mindset', and developing existing employees into change agents. For example, aluminium giant Norsk Hydro found an effective way of learning how to embark on the sustainability transformation journey. It invested in two-way learning exchanges between leaders from its strategy, innovation and sustainability areas and senior executives from other industries, leading to a sharper vision, deeper understanding of critical transformation skills and identification of unexpected collaboration opportunities.

4 Future-Fit Culture

Sustainability cannot be just a statement from top leadership, an investment in clean technology or a CSR report prepared by the communications team. In line with Meadows' (1999) categorisation of mindset as a powerful lever for systemic change, building a future-fit culture not only enables companies to effectively capture the potential benefits of the sustainability transition but, more importantly, equips them to credibly drive transformation in the wider system. For example, during the 2010s, Dutch beer giant Heineken deliberately created a sustainability movement by encouraging people across the organisation to propose, shape and lead sustainability initiatives. Activating and channelling this enormous source of latent energy made the new values visible and anchored the Brew a Better World culture that today is a critical driver of Heineken's EverGreen strategy for balanced growth. The strategy includes systemic commitments to have a carbon-neutral value chain by 2040, and ambitious targets on social justice and responsible consumption (Heineken, 2021).

5 Integration

Sustainability must be integrated into strategic and daily decision-making to effectively translate the sustainable culture and values into material impact and new growth. Stefano et al. (2018) claim that the contribution of human resources (HR) departments in facilitating more socially responsible and sustainable organisations remains unclear and presents a framework with which to classify the role that HR might play. Leading companies reflect their sustainability objectives in HR strategy and appraisal systems, making sustainability an integral part of target setting for business and operational units and tying ESG indicators to the remuneration and long-term incentives of leaders across the organisation. Building on previous Unilever CEO Paul Polman's promotion of purpose-driven values under his Sustainable Living Plan, new CEO Alan Jope introduced Unilever's Compass Strategy, engaging the entire organisation in translating sustainability strategy into business objectives across all areas of the company, such that it guides everyday business decisions and powers purpose-driven innovation and high-growth sustainable brands.

6 Innovation and Acceleration

The times when companies used to compete largely based on their in-house R&D capabilities and focussed much of their innovation on incremental improvements of their legacy business are long gone. Navigating today's fast-changing environment and the complexity of sustainability-related challenges, companies that emphasise open innovation, bringing in new capabilities, insights and expertise, are more likely to create radical reinvention and scale successfully (Inauen & Schenker-Wicki, 2012). Companies that aim to be at the forefront of the sustainability transition have started to set up corporate accelerators to in-source innovation capabilities through collaboration with start-ups, resulting in access to new technologies, industries, markets and customers, giving start-ups access to expertise and resources in exchange (Kohler, 2016; Moschner et al., 2019). This can range from Unilever's Foundry (Unilever Foundry, n.d.), an entire floor in its Southeast Asian headquarters in Singapore that is available for start-ups, to Microsoft or Amazon fuelling their innovation ecosystems through, respectively, their \$1 billion Climate Innovation and \$2 billion Climate Pledge Funds (Microsoft, n.d.; Amazon, n.d.).

7 Collaborations for New Growth

Capturing new growth opportunities while driving sustainability in society requires building purpose-driven and cross-sectoral collaborations. These can be supply chain–, sector- or issue-specific. For example, H&M, IKEA, Adidas and other founding members of the WWF-initiated Better Cotton Initiative (2021) created supply chain transparency and demand for sustainable cotton, now covering 2.2 million cotton farmers or 20 per cent of the world's cotton production. In Thailand, companies like CP Group, one of the largest agri-food companies in the country, engaged supply chain partners for education, training 27,000 rice farmers in the country on how to work with low-emission rice cultivation techniques, leading to a nearly 40 per cent reduction in the carbon footprint for white rice (Bangkok Post, 2022). The strongest collaborations are driven by opportunities to accelerate new growth, such as Yara and IBM collaborating to advance digital farming to enhance both the lives of farmers and the sustainability of farming, aiming to cover 150 million hectares or 10 per cent of the world's arable land (IBM, 2022).

While system innovation is frequently viewed as a threat by legacy industries, some businesses have realised that reinventing themselves and how they interact with customers may increase their success. One of those is consumer goods giant Unilever (2020), which increasingly uses systems thinking to drive the redesign of products and processes. The company has been vocal about the need for policymakers to support systemic changes, and it is leading advocacy and initiatives for change in the energy, water and agricultural systems that it forms part of. In Southeast Asia, Unilever is making efforts to address the region's plastic waste challenge. By creating demand for recycled materials, backed up by public commitments to halve its use of virgin plastics by 2025, and empowering and engaging the informal waste sector, the company is fuelling the development of a plastic collection and recycling ecosystem in Southeast Asia, with the objective to drive circular business models, reduce waste, improve lives and capture savings in the process. But while larger plastic containers fit this solution, finding circular solutions for the 40 billion smaller sachets Unilever sells annually continues to be a big and controversial challenge (Brock & Geddie, 2022; McVeigh & Holliani Cahya, 2022).

3.3 Future-Fit Mindsets

Getting citizens, policymakers, industry and scientists to come to a consensus in terms of the complex nature of sustainability challenges, as a precondition for collaboration for systemic change, is a process that requires effort and time. This is particularly true as it is increasingly recognised that a change of mind is required, a profound shift of awareness of the changes needed that is on the transformational level of a paradigm shift (Laininen, 2018). Political economist Polanyi (1944) already recognised the importance of mindset by defining transformation as a profound alteration of human mentalities that generates new institutions that in turn reconstruct the economy, the state and distributional relations. In line with Meadows' (1999) identification of the deep potential of paradigm and mindset change for systemic transformation, what paradigms and mindsets do we need to drive the right kind of systemic change? And how can we build these mindsets and amplify this powerful lever?

3.3.1 Shifting Paradigms

Kuhn coined the term 'paradigm shift' in 1962, referring to a shift in science from Newtonian to Einsteinian physics (Voulvoulis et al., 2022). Paradigm shifts occur when 'the anomalies and shortcomings of the current paradigm are repeatedly pointed out; proponents of the new paradigm speak loudly and with assurance about it and are placed into positions of visibility and power; and energy is focused on converting those people who are likely to be open-minded to the change' (p. 3). Unless due to some revolutionary innovation or discovery, the process of a paradigm shift is often triggered by a period of crisis or accumulation of anomalies. This leads to a phase of exploration and critical thinking, of challenging the status quo and finally of scaling the new paradigm and the models and systems that emerge from it.

Interesting parallels exist between trends today and events that led to previous major shifts in mindset. The European Enlightenment, following a period of religious intolerance and polarisation in the first half of the 1600s that resulted in Europe's most devastating Thirty-Year War, triggered a loss of faith in the church and monarchy, the institutions that dominated society at that time. The scientific revolution brought critical thinking, while discoveries from geographic exploration at the time fed curiosity and brought new ideas, the exchange of which was fuelled thanks to urbanisation, the spread of the press and increased literacy. This empowered society to reinvent itself and change its purpose so as to improve the human condition on Earth rather than serving religion in the hope of an afterlife.

Today's world is in a climate of (geo)political polarisation, growing social inequity, failing institutions and, as mentioned before, a lack of public trust in government, NGOs and media (Edelman Trust Institute, 2023). The situation is further destabilised by the impacts of the recent Covid-19 pandemic and the ever-clearer disrupting effects of the climate crisis. Coupled with rapid technological progress and connectivity, the conditions seem right for Enlightenment 2.0, a recalibration of paradigms: a different understanding of welfare, progress and freedom. While the list in Table 4 does not pretend to be exhaustive and universal, and the changes are gradual rather than absolute, it does show ten shifts in paradigms and mindsets, in line with Enlightenment 2.0, that we see emerging.

Enlightenment 2.0 calls for an open-minded mindset, characterised by contextual curiosity, the effort to understand the broad spectrum of information that makes up the full picture, sometimes coming from antagonistic sources, and the willingness to question existing paradigms. This mindset can be supported by skill development in the areas of empathic listening, conflict resolution, shared visioning and collaboration and the creation of podia for civilised dialogue, today's equivalent of the English coffee houses or the French and central European salons during the first Enlightenment, where facts and feelings can be heard, identified and considered when discussing and designing collective action. The 'light' in Enlightenment 2.0 is the light of reason of the future-forward mindset, of comprehending our place on Earth in a new system more befitting the emerging paradigms.

3.3.2 The Dynamics of Mindset Change

While literature generally suggests that cognitive, emotional and cultural factors bring about paradigm shift and the accompanying mindset change, the role of emotions in psychological change garners particular attention (Frijda et al., 2000; Wood, 2000; Marsella & Gratch, 2002). In line with this, McPhearson et al. (2016) argue that inspirational visions can be key components for behavioural change and action. More information transparency on, for example, life-cycle impact, hidden subsidies or the societal business case could be a cognitive driver of systemic change. However, combined with deeply emotional, spiritual or eye-opening experiences, it could also change the social sentiment and trigger cross-stakeholder empathy and collaboration. This was the case when Apollo astronaut Bill Anders took the Earthrise photograph from the Apollo

Table 4 Ten emerging paradigms for a sustainable twenty-first century.

(a)

Fading paradigms (legacy)	Emerging paradigms (new)
Anthropocentric worldview: mankind is superior to nature. Nature can be exploited for economic value because it is 'infinite' and abundant, leading to reductionist and anthropocentric policies, and regulations often with (negative) unintended consequences.	**Systemic worldview:** everything is connected. Mankind cannot survive without nature, whose resources are limited. We work with nature, not against it, to optimise nature's capacity to provide us with valuable natural services, requiring holistic, integrated, interdisciplinary thinking and policy.
Shareholder capitalism: the purpose of business is to optimise economic capital/GDP growth and risk-return for capital investors. Sustainability and economic growth are trade-offs and should be evaluated from a risk and return perspective.	**Stakeholder capitalism:** the purpose of business is to optimise shared value for all stakeholders, recognise the value of economic, natural, human and social capital in balance, and focus on societal, global and intergenerational fairness and equity. Profit without purpose leads to poverty.
Efficiency-orientation: optimisation of Business as Usual assets through cost-saving and incremental innovation.	**Impact-orientation:** reinvention of systems to optimise regeneration, impact and new value creation. The need to solve our biggest societal challenges constitutes the biggest commercial opportunity of our age.
Linear Economy: the take-make-use-waste principle. The more we produce and consume, the more economic value is created. We make excessive use of primary raw materials and fossil energy sources (take), make products as cheaply as possible (make), use these products briefly (use) and throw them away after usage (waste).	**Circular Economy:** the borrow-make-use-return principle. We decouple economic growth from material use. We use secondary raw materials (borrow), design and create products aimed at extending their lifespan, using renewable energy, keeping last stage in mind (make), use products longer and make them last (use), and return products to the producer for their next life, or let natural materials decompose in ecological systems (return).
Colonialist: despite the end of colonialism, systemic racism still exists within and between societies. Globalisation through offshoring and migration provides access to cheaper production and bigger markets for economic gain.	**Pluralist:** diversity is a source of richness, innovation and resilience. Minority wisdom through for example the enabling of local stakeholders' stewardship of lands and communities, can strengthen local and global resilience.

(b)

Externalities are 'commons': societal and environmental cost of business activity is the responsibility of governments & regulators.	**Extended Producer Responsibility:** businesses are responsible for their societal and environmental externalities.
Short-term materialism: people seek material possessions and short-term gratification for status and happiness. Carpe Diem.	**Long-term well-being:** once basic material needs are taken care of, spiritual well-being (experiences, reflection, development, identities, relationships, purpose and values) gives more long-term satisfaction than additional material wealth. Know Thyself.
Power in size: economic, political and opinion-shaping power is with the establishment of big business, government and religion. But the power imbalance risks leading to sentiments of disenfranchisement among 'ordinary' people.	**Power in connected numbers:** power is shifting to increasingly activist social-media-empowered masses. But misinformation, manipulation, polarisation and security issues are causing a reconsideration of the adequate level of government and corporate control of digital media.
Individualist: individualism and competition optimise wealth creation, but diversity increases complexity.	**Collectivist:** intelligent self-moderation and civilised collaborative behaviour create well-being for all.
Techno-utopia: human ingenuity and technology will come to our rescue and solve our problems.	**Humanity:** technology can be an enabler, but we need to bring empathy back into decision-making to solve our problems.

spacecraft on Christmas Eve in 1968 (Anders, 1968). Seeing the beauty and the vulnerability of our planet from space was the beginning of a change in our relationship with the world and our understanding of our shared fate (see Figure 9).

In addition to the cognitive, emotional and cultural dimensions, we would like to add a fourth dimension: the leadership itself of the change process. Transformative leaders build movements, energising stakeholders by creating a sense of urgency, helping them build a rich, joint vision of the challenge at hand and inviting them to reflect on how individual stakeholders' purposes align with the shared purpose. Transformative leaders deliberately lead their employees and other stakeholders, such as investors or consumers, to new paradigms. When former Unilever CEO Paul Polman, days after taking the helm of the multinational, famously announced to shareholders that Unilever would move from trimestral to annual financial reporting, not only did he signal and set

Figure 9 The Earthrise image: creating shared fate and responsibility.

expectations towards investors but he also catalysed a longer-term mindset and ignited a sense of purpose with his employees and supply chain partners (Skapinker & Daneshkhu, 2016).

Another company leveraging its size and credibility to drive a consumer paradigm shift is Ikea. After being one of the first large retailers to ban incandescent light bulbs in favour of the hugely more efficient LED lights, it is now replacing its famous meatballs, of which it sells more than a billion per year, with plant-based versions. According to the Sierra Club, the production of a plant-based burger generates 12 times fewer GHG emissions than one made of beef, uses 50 times less water and requires 20 times less land (Steinbauer, 2020); thus, Ikea's swap will help the company meet its objective of being climate-positive by 2030. But, more importantly, it will encourage its customers to adopt healthier consumption patterns for them and the planet.

Given the all-encompassing nature of systemic change and learning from the challenges and failures described in Section 2, for successful implementation, it is essential to align the cognitive and emotional mindsets not only of the decision-making stakeholders but also of the citizens affected by it. We will therefore explore the reciprocal dynamics of mindset change between decision-makers and stakeholders, particularly citizens.

3.3.2.1 Widespread Mindset Shifts – Manipulation versus Engagement

Digital technology can be used to influence paradigms, mindsets and behaviours. Gladwell (2000) describes in his book *The Tipping Point* that an idea can exist underneath the surface in a society or among a small group of people and then, seemingly overnight, suddenly erupt everywhere, changing the way an entire society acts or thinks. Or drinks . . . As the benefits of oat milk compared to cow milk went viral on social media early on in the Covid-19 pandemic, consumers in the USA turned to oat milk, causing a 478 per cent rise in oat milk sales in the second week of March 2020 compared to the same week in 2019 (Iversen, 2020). Social media making indiscriminate sharing so effortless carries the risk of conditioning people to follow trends and support opinions in shallow and frivolous ways, and sometimes influence is lost as fast as it was gained. Even though this is not new in sustainability circles, one current online phenomenon that can influence mindsets towards more sustainable models is de-influencing, where influencers – content creators in a specific niche or with specific expertise, a large online following and the ability to influence their audience – encourage their followers not to buy or do something as an antidote to consumerism and our linear way of living. The hashtag's popularity – currently 300 million views on TikTok and growing – makes it part of the internet discourse at large. Almost half of Gen Z (born between 1996 and 2012) makes purchase decisions based on influencer recommendations, so de-influencing could well become part of the wider mindset shift needed to address systemic issues (Global Fashion Agenda, 2023). If de-influencing moves beyond being another social media trend, it has the power to mark a shift in the current cultural zeitgeist and help catalyse the tipping point from short-term materialism to a paradigm focussed on long-term well-being.

But, besides social media trends, recent history has also shown examples at the other end of the spectrum of how digital technologies can amplify and accelerate deep mindset change, sometimes with radical consequences for the relationship between corporations, governments and citizens, as several Middle Eastern and North African regimes learnt when they were toppled by digitally connected citizens during the Arab spring.

A distrust of large foundations, science and governments and a fragmenting social fabric characterise today's society. Facts are viewed as subjective; even the most provable and basic ones are disputed (Wardle & Derakhshan, 2017). In this post-truth era, ushered in by US claims surrounding the Iraq war (Bayoumi, 2023), objective facts seem less influential in shaping public opinion and political views than alternative facts based on personal biases and emotion. In the digital age, there is always a danger of manipulation of public opinion through information disorder, such as the prevalence of spreading disinformation and fake news. The Cambridge Analytica scandal showed how digital platforms can be used to manipulate public sentiment in less noble ways. In a defensive move against the power of social media, several governments including Russia, Turkey, Indonesia and China have taken steps to regulate and control its use, while at the same time leveraging its manipulative potential for their benefit.

Several scholars have argued that to negate the force of information disorder, it is essential for opinion-makers, scientists and influencers to provide society with reliable information and to focus on responsible science (Vogt, 2021; Tanwar et al., 2022). This seems to be in line with the system lever described by Meadows (1999) as the structure of information flows: who does and does not have access to specific information at specific places influences how people behave or don't behave, based on that information. However, similar to the erroneous belief that more growth would solve many of the problems caused by growth, it is not simply strengthening of the responsible scientific information flow that will mitigate the problem of alternative facts. Rather, what is needed is de-polarisation, relaxing defensive attitudes and reviving the willingness to acknowledge all voices. This requires platforms for constructive dialogue. The importance of constructive dialogue in conflict resolution and de-polarisation has been widely discussed (Yankelovich, 1999; Ropers, 2004; Ercan, 2017). However, accelerated by Covid-19, large parts of our communication have moved online, radically changing the nature of interaction and necessitating a rethinking of public engagement and dialogue online. In more open societies, social media still plays an important role in shaping public consciousness and enabling citizens to engage with politics in new ways (Miller & Vaccari, 2020). But this is not always a straightforward process. Many governments are exploring ways for technology to enable constructive stakeholder dialogue while finding a balance between protecting citizens' rights and ensuring public safety. For example, through its minister of digital affairs, Audrey Tang (2019), Taiwan has arguably been among the most progressive at introducing digital democracy, allowing connectedness to facilitate input rather than conflict, promoting citizen-led fact-checking and public opinion collation, and applying cyber security for civil society.

3.3.2.2 Citizen Power – Activating a Virtuous Cycle

Besides citizen power nudged on by governmental influence, we see more and more frequently that societal action born of intrinsic motivation can also influence corporate or government decision-makers. Intrinsic motivation can be cognitive, emotional or value-based (Schulz & Siriwardane, 2015). For example, in the Netherlands, 900 citizens together with the Urgenda Foundation sued the Dutch government, demanding that it do more to prevent global climate change, in the first-ever climate case. They won in 2019 and inspired other climate litigations worldwide (Leijten, 2019). Globally, citizens unite in Extinction Rebellion, a non-partisan and non-violent network to bring forth a true sense of urgency for the climate crisis, organising citizens' assemblies and promoting participative democracy using disruptive direct action (Extinction Rebellion, 2022).

In the case of the following example, intrinsic motivation is values- and emotions-based. After years of non-participatory decision-making by the local government, in which Jakarta's poor kampung settlements were demolished to make way for flood protection measures, in the face of eviction threats the increasingly marginalised citizens of Tongkol formed the Ciliwung River Community, a forum of about 1,000 households, to facilitate the discussion of strategies to claim back their community. They rebuilt their homes 5 metres from the waterway, created clear access along the riverbank, cleaned up their river, planted trees, set up a community-wide composting and recycling scheme, encouraged self-sufficiency with vertical vegetable gardens and became 'guardians of the river', attracting tourism to a part of Jakarta that was largely hidden from the public gaze before (Dovey et al., 2019). The Tongkol citizens showed the local government that citizen empowerment could lead to community-based upgrading of urban systems and an eco-friendlier future for the city. They influenced the approach to flood management in Jakarta and beyond.

Empowering citizens through engagement and information can start a virtuous cycle, enabling them to understand the bigger system perspective, to think critically, to realise their responsibility and potential, and to keep companies, institutions and politicians in check (McGann et al., 2021). Climate change will have unavoidable impacts on populations and urban systems, especially in Asia where many large cities are exposed. The example from Jakarta illustrates that decision-making processes should be inclusive and participatory, inviting the citizens that are most affected by climate hazards to play an active role in determining how best to avoid them, build resilience and pave the way for systemic change. Policymakers that proactively evolve participation beyond consultation through joint visioning processes, gathering input from citizens and enabling more inclusive decision-making processes, such as policy co-design or participatory budgeting, build the kind of stakeholder support that is essential to any systemic change or sustainability transition (Angheloiu & Tennant, 2020).

Following the principles of *The Wisdom of Crowds* (Surowiecki, 2004), yearly more than 2.3 million volunteers worldwide collect data in thousands of biodiversity projects. This so-called citizen science, in which the public is involved in scientific research, spans multiple disciplines such as psychology, astronomy, ecology and environmental science, biodiversity and tourism. The strength of engaging citizens in science lies in the potential for getting new and outlying perspectives that could be crucial in addressing the complex, wicked problems of our time (Rowbotham et al., 2019). Most of all, citizen science creates a sense of inclusiveness and has the opportunity to translate global problems to a local scale and reality; this is much needed in the current post-truth era.

3.3.3 Educating Mindful Leaders

The inability of our institutions to avoid war, banking crises, business and religious scandals, inequality and climate action failure has eroded trust in capitalism, business and government leaders to the lowest level in decades. As a result, a leadership change is taking place. Traditional leaders that are uncomfortable in the VUCA environment are receding into the historic paradigms and values they are comfortable with, such as the pursuit of short-term profit. At the other end of the spectrum, a new generation of leaders who are mentally and functionally equipped to drive change in a VUCA world is emerging.

Models emerging from the scientific Enlightenment and industrialisation have brought a lot of economic growth. However, in our singular focus on GDP growth, we have forgotten about the importance of the quality and distribution of GDP. We need a more widespread recognition that well-being for individuals and society emerges from a balance of natural, social and economic capital. We must build models and systems to satisfy society's needs that stay within environmental boundaries and don't erode societal foundations. How can we embed this vision and future-fit mindset in leaders to help them make better decisions in their personal realm, in their public or business organisations and, most importantly, in the bigger systems they participate in?

Business schools are pivotal in educating and equipping future leaders as agents of change. To change the systems in which we operate, we need to equip our future leaders with the mindset, skills and tools to drive systemic change on a playing field that is becoming increasingly VUCA. This requirement adds a whole new layer to the traditional functional areas of management education.

Sterman & Sweeney (2007) and Valerdi & Rouse (2010) concluded that systems thinking performance, even by highly educated people, can be poor. This is consistent with research by Palmberg et al. (2017) and Ndaruhutse et al. (2019) revealing that, currently, education does not adequately develop systems thinking competence. It coincides with calls for policymakers to move systems thinking competencies higher up the educational agenda (International Commission on Financing Global Education Opportunity, 2016). Other authors suggest that incorporating systems thinking in education could benefit students by helping them acquire a more holistic view of and a mindset that facilitates addressing sustainability challenges (Hofman-Bergholm, 2018; Žalėnienė &

Pereira, 2021). In addition, systems thinking supports interdisciplinarity by building shared thinking space and knowledge that cuts across the boundaries of various disciplines (Barile & Saviano, 2021). It also encourages public engagement with science through intentional, meaningful interactions that provide opportunities for mutual learning between scientists and members of the public and thus promote familiarity with a breadth of perspectives, frames and worldviews (Stave, 2002).

The Sasin School of Management in Bangkok believes that in an increasingly VUCA world, successful leaders must continuously transform themselves, their organisations and the systems in which they operate in sustainable and profitable ways. Sasin addresses this need by teaching mindful leadership, which identifies six interrelated capabilities (see Figure 10) (Van der Zanden, 2023):

1. **Contextual mindfulness**: the humility and critical thinking needed to seek and make meaning of intelligence from a range of sources, to connect the dots between disparate data points while being aware of filters and biases, and to engage with trends before they become clear and present.
2. **Future consciousness**: the ability to imagine the future through divergent thinking, using multiple lenses and scenarios, while applying multigenerational empathy and agency over the long-term futures of humans and society.
3. **Systems range**: the sense of leadership responsibility and stakeholder empathy that is needed not only to run high-performing organisations but

Figure 10 Mindful leadership skills, critical for sustainability transformation.

Box 5 Sufficiency Economy

The sufficiency economy philosophy is based on the Theravada Buddhist principles of moderation (Pho praman), reasonableness (Mi het phon) and risk-resilience (Phumikhum kan nai tua), providing strategic guidance for companies in their aim to be responsible, sustainable businesses. It applies the Buddhist practice of mindfulness in business decision-making, improving systemic understanding and stakeholder awareness, and contributing to prudent risk management and shared value creation:

- Moderation is the prudent management of risks based on normal, sound business grounds. Moderation provides a balanced approach towards stakeholder relationships and risk–reward opportunities: balance is the path of virtue, a middle way that provides a buffer against risk, where no one stakeholder can trump the interests of the others, and which prevents succumbing to irrational exuberance and market distortion.
- Reasonableness is driven by a win–win mentality that builds trust, mutuality and cooperation rather than competition. It calls for understanding the full consequences of our conduct for other stakeholders, not only in the short term but over the long term as well.
- The risk-resilience of a company and its surrounding system, and thus the company's present value, is increased in the sufficiency economy by building financial, human, social and reputational capital through the application of moderation and the avoidance of unreasonable relationships.

The sufficiency economy promotes two-character virtues, which are particularly relevant in today's crisis of distrust, polarisation, greenwashing and misinformation – knowledge (kwam ru) and integrity (khunatham) – as essential pillars for quality of management and constructive stakeholder relationships.

Mindful leaders consider their actions' long-term future and system-level consequences, which requires knowledge and judgement, not passion, in making decisions. Integrity, the moral faculty of self-control and regard for others, requires deep reflection on ourselves, our values, beliefs and biases in relationship to our stakeholders' potential, needs and values. It is built through good governance, transparency and keeping promises.

also to co-shape and enrich the systems in which we operate by understanding the relationships between the components and actors in a system and foreseeing the intended and unintended ripple effect of one's interventions in that system.

4. **Cross-collaborative competence**: the ability and capacity to successfully engineer and lead transformative collaborations with non-traditional change partners, mobilised through a compelling shared vision and trusted relationships.
5. **Radical impact agility**: the ability to keep a relentless focus on delivering radical impact, despite being surrounded by VUCA, deploying disruptive intent, an entrepreneurial bias for action and the mental and physical agility to continuously question the status quo and to explore, develop and evolve radical new models of impact and value creation.
6. **Purpose**: the self-knowledge, integrity, moral compass and clarity of purpose that will inspire others to reimagine and align their activities with the bigger purpose.

Integrated into the teaching of mindful leadership are the principles of the sufficiency economy, an ethical philosophy introduced in 1997 by Thailand's King Bhumibol Adulyadej as an alternative to an economy of excess risk that had caused the economic crisis of that time. His Majesty's vision was of an economy that is sufficient rather than excessive, with a concern for gradual, holistic development across all of society, not just for affluent urban elites, and that proceeds with care, economy and foresight to prevent mistakes (Mongsawad, 2012). Numerous sectors have successfully adopted the philosophy in Thailand, most notably the financial sector, improving stakeholder satisfaction and reducing both risk and cost of capital.

In his address at the leadership forum The Performance Theatre, former professor of Indo-Tibetan Buddhist studies at Columbia University Bob Thurman (2014) explained how the Buddhist belief in reincarnation translates into a powerful transgenerational motivation for sustainability. As we deteriorate our natural and social environment, we deteriorate the conditions we will have to live with after reincarnation. Only when we leave the world in a better state than we found it do we have a chance to reach Enlightenment.

Agricultural societies worldwide survive by the grace of the interdependency between man and nature. Especially in smaller-scale agricultural communities, this has translated into the concept of stewardship, living sustainably in the environment and preserving natural capital for the next generations. Eastern wisdom traditions have a deep-rooted conviction that everything is connected and that all forms of life are equally sacred and deserve to be preserved. The paradigm at the base of the Western mindset, namely that nature was created in the service of man and is there for man to exploit, might have accelerated the destruction of natural capital for economic gains. But progressing awareness and insight into the need to restore natural capital and build its capacity as our ally against many of the challenges we face as a society is giving rise to a boom in regenerative practices, and interest in biomimicry.

Irrespective of the underlying religion, life philosophy or wisdom tradition, the right thing to do is to educate more mindful leaders to empathically understand the bigger picture and equip them to lead the (re)design of the systems that we live in to create future societies that are more in harmony with themselves and with nature.

Final Thoughts

The size and the increasing urgency of humanity's environmental and social challenges require a radical reinvention of the critical systems that satisfy our needs. Of course, the transformation of complex, embedded systems is complicated. However, deliberate efforts to create the conditions that are necessary to strengthen future-fit mindsets and collaboration among stakeholders are crucial points of intervention, enabling systems to emerge that produce a new kind of growth that will increase well-being for all without eroding natural or social capital.

Mindset change and collaboration in a fast-changing world plagued by polarisation, distrust and failing institutions are difficult but possible if we strengthen platforms for constructive dialogue and engagement, encourage stakeholders to build a shared understanding of, and vision for, the bigger picture surrounding our shared challenges, and create the space for ourselves as individuals and as connected members of society to question the paradigms that underlie our behaviours and decisions.

The looming environmental and social crises could accelerate Enlightenment 2.0 if we decide to channel the forces of change for the better. Navigating this grand challenge and the corresponding opportunities will show us whether more liberal or authoritarian regimes will deliver systemic change more quickly and more sustainably. We will learn whether businesses, governments or citizens will be the most influential driving force in bringing the remaining stakeholders together for collaborative transformation towards future-fit systems and how the conditions for such collaboration can be improved. Nevertheless, the most profound driver of positive change will be our ability to become more mindful and, collectively, to respectfully align our mindsets on the type of world we want to build. We are in this together, as Carl Sagan (1994) eloquently said in *Pale Blue Dot*:

> The earth is the only world known so far to harbour life. There is nowhere else, at least in the near future, to which our species could migrate. Visit, yes. Settle, not yet. Like it or not, for the moment, the earth is where we make our

stand ... To me, it underscores our responsibility to deal more kindly with one another and to preserve and cherish the pale blue dot, the only home we've ever known. (p. 13)

Systems thinking, mindfulness and transformation dynamics are still under-researched and under-prioritised in education. Yet, educational institutions play a pivotal role in equipping the leaders who will shape humanity's future with the mindsets, skills and tools they will need to drive radical, positive change. Our mindful decisions and our ability to change in the next 30 years will determine our collective fate in the next 300 years and more.

References

Abboud, L. (2018, 7 October). UK farmers prepare for overhaul to farm subsidies after Brexit. *Financial Times*.

ACI Worldwide. (2021, 29 March). Global real-time payments transactions surge by 41 percent in 2020 as COVID-19 pandemic accelerates shift to digital payments – new ACI Worldwide research reveals. https://bit.ly/48s5L14.

Allenbach-Ammann, J. (2022, 20 October). EU Commission to facilitate state support for R&D investments. *Euractiv*. https://bit.ly/3Psoz7F.

Amazon. (n.d.). *The Climate Pledge Fund*. https://bit.ly/3RqhRS9.

Amrute, S., Khera, R., & Willems, A. (2020). Aadhaar and the creation of barriers to welfare. *Interactions*, *27*(6), 76–9.

Anders, B. (1968). Earthrise. Image. NASA. https://bit.ly/3LTaUp6.

Angheloiu, C., & Tennant, M. (2020). Urban futures: systemic or system changing interventions? A literature review using Meadows' leverage points as analytical framework. *Cities*, *104*, 102808.

Angheloiu, C., Sheldrick, L., Tennant, M., & Chaudhuri, G. (2020). Future tense: harnessing design futures methods to facilitate young people's exploration of transformative change for sustainability. *World Futures Review*, *12*(1), 104–22.

Arora, B., Singhal, A., & Mahavidyalaya, K. (2013). A comprehensive literature on impacts of microfinance. *Indian Journal of Economics & Business*, *16*(1), 121–33.

Association of Southeast Asian Nations (ASEAN). (2020). *ASEAN Integrated Food Security (AIFS) Framework and Strategic Plan of Action on Food Security in the ASEAN Region (SPA-FS) 2021–2025*. https://bit.ly/3Ly1Sh6.

Balch, O. (2020, 8 December). The curse of 'white oil': electric vehicles' dirty secret. *Guardian*.

Bangkok Post. (2022). C.P. Group's climate smart agriculture: balancing food security amidst climate and geopolitical volatility. *Bangkok Post*.

Bar-On, Y. M., Phillips, R., & Milo, R. (2018). The biomass distribution on Earth. *Proceedings of the National Academy of Sciences*, *115*(25), 6506–11.

Barile, S., & Saviano, M. (2021). Interdisciplinary systems thinking for a new scientific paradigm: toward a re-founding of human values. In G. Minati (ed.), *Multiplicity and Interdisciplinarity*, 17–39. Cham: Springer.

Barling, D., Lang, T., & Caraher, M. (2002). Joined-up food policy? The trials of governance, public policy and the food system. *Social Policy & Administration*, *36*, 556–74.

Barton, J., Davies, L., Dooley, B., et al. (2018). Transition pathways for a UK low-carbon electricity system: comparing scenarios and technology implications. *Renewable and Sustainable Energy Reviews, 82*(3), 2779–90.

Baykara, S. Z. (2018). Hydrogen: a brief overview on its sources, production and environmental impact. *International Journal of Hydrogen Energy, 43*(23), 10605–14.

Bayoumi, M. (2023, 14 March). The Iraq war started the post-truth era. And America is to blame. *Guardian.*

Bennis, W. G., & O'Toole, J. (2005). How business schools have lost their way. *Harvard Business Review, 83*(5), 96–104.

Benyus, J. M. (2002). *Biomimicry: Innovation Inspired by Nature.* New York: HarperCollins.

Better Cotton Initiative. (2021). *2021 Annual Report.* https://bit.ly/3PPuUeM.

Biermann, F. (2021). The future of 'environmental' policy in the Anthropocene: time for a paradigm shift. *Environmental Politics, 30*(1–2), 61–80.

Bonn Challenge. (2011). *About the Challenge.* www.bonnchallenge.org/about.

Brock, J., & Geddie, J. (2022, 22 June). *Unilever's Plastic Playbook.* Reuters. https://bit.ly/3t7A50D.

Brown University. (2021). *Profits of War: Corporate Beneficiaries of the Post-9/11 Pentagon Spending Surge.* https://watson.brown.edu/costsofwar/papers/2021/ProfitsOfWar.

Bryson, J. M., Crosby, B. C., & Stone, M. M. (2006). The design and implementation of cross-sector collaborations: propositions from the literature. *Public Administration Review, 66*, 44–55.

Bryson, J. M., Crosby, B. C., & Stone, M. M. (2015). Designing and implementing cross-sector collaborations: needed and challenging. *Public Administration Review, 75*, 647–63.

Capgemini Consulting. (2015). *When Digital Disruption Strikes: How Can Incumbents Respond?* https://bit.ly/3RvkQso.

Capra, F., & Luisi, P. L. (2014). *The Systems View of Life: A Unifying Vision.* Cambridge: Cambridge University Press.

Carroll, A. B. (2016). Carroll's pyramid of CSR: taking another look. *International Journal of Corporate Social Responsibility, 1*(3). https://doi.org/10.1186/s40991-016-0004-6.

Celis-Morales, C. A., Lyall, D. M., Welsh, P., et al. (2017). Association between active commuting and incident cardiovascular disease, cancer, and mortality: prospective cohort study. *BMJ, 357*(1456). https://doi.org/10.1136/bmj.j1456.

Chan, H.-Y. (2013). Crisis politics in authoritarian regimes: how crises catalyse changes under the state–society interactive framework. *Journal of Contingencies*

and Crisis Management, 21(4), 200–10. https://doi.org/10.1111/1468-5973
.12024.

Chen, J., & Xu, Y. (2017). Information manipulation and reform in authoritarian
regimes. *Political Science Research and Methods, 5*, 163–78.

China Dialogue. (2006). China issues first 'green GDP' report. https://bit.ly/
3PvFJB8.

Choi, E., & Seiger, A. (2020). *Catalyzing Capital for the Transition toward
Decarbonization: Blended Finance and Its Way Forward*. Stanford, CA:
Stanford Sustainable Finance Initiative. https://bit.ly/46lqqBN.

Circularity Gap Reporting Initiative (CGRI). (2023). *The Circularity Gap
Report 2023*. www.circularity-gap.world/2023.

City of Amsterdam. (2020). *Policy: Circular Economy*. www.amsterdam.nl/en/
policy/sustainability/circular-economy/.

Clarke, A., & Crane, A. (2018). Cross-sector partnerships for systemic change:
systematized literature review and agenda for further research. *Journal of
Business Ethics, 150*(2), 303–13.

Connolly, K. (2022, 30 August). Germany's €9 train tickets scheme 'saved 1.8m
tons of CO2 emissions'. *Guardian*.

Cornwell, S. (2021, 22 April). Tax breaks for fossil fuels 'a disgrace,' Greta
Thunberg tells U.S. Congress. Reuters. https://bit.ly/48zlYBt.

Corporate Europe Observatory. (2020). *CAP vs Farm to Fork: Will We Pay
Billions to Destroy, or to Support Biodiversity, Climate, and Farmers?*
https://bit.ly/3LA1aQx.

Corporate Europe Observatory. (2022). *Agribusiness Lobby against EU Farm
to Fork Strategy Amplified by Ukraine War*. https://bit.ly/3RvmHxm.

D'Aveni, R. A. (1999). Strategic supremacy through disruption and dominance.
Sloan Management Review, 40, 127–35.

Dalberg (S. Totapally, P. Sonderegger, P. Rao, J. Gosselt and G. Gupta). (2019).
State of Aadhaar: A People's Perspective. 2019 Edition. https://bit.ly/
460tvHX.

Danone. (2017). Regenerative agriculture. www.danone.com/impact/planet/
regenerative-agriculture.html.

De Grauwe, P. (2017). External limits of capitalism. In *The Limits of the
Market: The Pendulum Between Government and Market*, trans. A. Asbury,
11–18. Oxford: Oxford University Press.

Dorninger, C., Abson, D. J., Apetrei, C. I., et al. (2020). Leverage points for
sustainability transformation: a review on interventions in food and energy
systems. *Ecological Economics, 171*, 106570.

Dovey, K., Cook, B., & Achmadi, A. (2019). Contested riverscapes in Jakarta:
flooding, forced eviction and urban image. *Space and Polity, 23*(3), 265–82.

Doyle, M. (2002). From change novice to change expert: issues of learning, development and support. *Personnel Review, 31,* 465–81.

Edelman Trust Institute. (2023). *2023 Edelman Trust Barometer: Global Report.* https://bit.ly/3RxR2eP.

Ellen MacArthur Foundation. (2022). *The Global Commitment 2022.* https://ellenmacarthurfoundation.org/global-commitment-2022/overview.

Ellen MacArthur Foundation. (2023). Why buy light bulbs when you can buy light? *Signify.* https://bit.ly/3RvYZkS.

Ercan, S. A. (2017). From polarisation to pluralisation: a deliberative approach to illiberal cultures. *International Political Science Review, 38,* 114–27.

EUcalls. (2022, 22 March). What are the basics of the European Green Deal? https://eucalls.net/blog/the-basics-of-the-european-green-deal.

European Commission, Directorate-General for Research and Innovation. (2021). *EU Missions: Concrete Solutions for Our Greatest Challenges.* Luxembourg: Publications Office of the European Union.

European Union. (2020). *Farm to Fork Strategy: For a Fair, Healthy and Environmentally-Friendly Food System.* https://bit.ly/46ETB2Y.

Extinction Rebellion. (2022). *Global Support Mid-Year Report 2022.* https://cloud.organise.earth/s/GffoecgWHFa45Pc.

Fawcett, S. E., McCarter, M. W., Fawcett, A. M., Webb, G. S., & Magnan, G. M. (2015). Why supply chain collaboration fails: the socio-structural view of resistance to relational strategies. *Supply Chain Management, 20,* 648–63.

Fischer, J., & Riechers, M. (2018). A leverage points perspective on sustainability. *People and Nature, 1*(1), 115–20.

Food and Agriculture Organization of the United Nations (FAO). (2020). *Global Forest Resources Assessment.* www.fao.org/3/ca9825en/ca9825en.pdf.

Food and Agriculture Organization of the United Nations (FAO). (2021). *A Multi-Billion-Dollar Opportunity: Repurposing Agricultural Support to Transform Food Systems.* www.fao.org/documents/card/en/c/CB6683EN.

Foxon, T. J., Reed, M. S., & Stringer, L. C. (2009). Governing long-term social-ecological change: what can the adaptive management and transition management approaches learn from each other? *Environmental Policy and Governance, 19*(1), 3–20.

Freeman, C. (1991). Networks of innovators: a synthesis of research issues. *Research Policy, 20*(5), 499–514.

Freiberg, D., Rogers, J., & Serafeim, G. (2020). *How ESG Issues Become Financially Material to Corporations and Their Investors.* Harvard Business School Accounting & Management Unit Working Paper, 20-056. www.hbs.edu/faculty/Pages/item.aspx?num=57161.

Friedman, M. (1970, 13 September). A Friedman doctrine: the social responsibility of business is to increase its profits. *New York Times*.

Frijda, N. H., Manstead, A. S., & Bem, S. (eds.) (2000). *Emotions and Beliefs: How Feelings Influence Thoughts*. Cambridge: Cambridge University Press.

Frohlich, T. C., Comen, E., & Suneson, G. (2019, 16 May). 15 commercial products invented by the military include GPS, duct tape and Silly Putty. *USA Today*. https://bit.ly/48CgVA3.

Geels, F. W. (2005). Processes and patterns in transitions and system innovations: refining the co-evolutionary multi-level perspective. *Technological Forecasting and Social Change*, *72*, 681–96.

Gilley, B. (2012). Authoritarian environmentalism and China's response to climate change. *Environmental Politics*, *21*, 287–307.

Gladwell, M. (2000). *The Tipping Point: How Little Things Can Make a Big Difference*. Boston, MA: Little Brown.

Global Fashion Agenda. (2023, 3 March). The impact of deinfluencing on the fashion industry. https://bit.ly/46aRww3.

Goh, J., Pfeffer, J., & Zenios, S. (2015). The relationship between workplace stressors and mortality and health costs in the United States. *Management Science*, *62*(2), 608–28.

Good Food Institute. (2022). *2021 State of Global Policy Report. With Highlights from the First Half of 2022*. https://gfi.org/wp-content/uploads/2022/10/POL22005_State-of-Global-Policy-Report.pdf.

Graça, P., & Camarinha-Matos, L. M. (2017). Performance indicators for collaborative business ecosystems: literature review and trends. *Technological Forecasting and Social Change*, *116*, 237–55.

Greenwald, M. (2023, 27 January). The challenge of chief sustainability officers: creating a new mindset throughout an entire global organization. *Forbes*. https://bit.ly/46dULmm.

Grunwald, A. (2007). Working towards sustainable development in the face of uncertainty and incomplete knowledge. *Journal of Environmental Policy & Planning*, *9*(3–4), 245–62.

Hand, D., Ringel, B., & Danel, A. (2022). *GIINsight: Sizing the Impact Investing Market: 2022*. Global Impact Investing Network (GIIN). https://bit.ly/48ua6AC.

Hanemaaijer, A., Kishna, M., Brink, H., et al. (2021), *Netherlands Integral Circular Economy Report 2021: English Summary*. The Hague: PBL Netherlands Environmental Assessment Agency. https://bit.ly/45nNUFM.

Heaton, H. (1937). Financing the Industrial Revolution. *Bulletin of the Business Historical Society*, *11*(1), 1–10.

Heineken. (2021, 22 April). Heiniken launches 2030 Brew a Better World ambitions. https://bit.ly/45l0VQ5.

Helliwell, J. F., Layard, R., Sachs, J. D., et al. (2022). *World Happiness Report 2022*. New York: Sustainable Development Solutions Network, powered by Gallup World Poll data. https://bit.ly/48zkNlA.

Hellström, J. (2009). Mobile phones for good governance: challenges and way forward. Draft discussion paper. www.w3.org/2008/10/MW4D_WS/papers/hellstrom_gov.pdf.

Hickman, R., & Banister, D. (2009). Techno-optimism: progress towards CO2 reduction targets in transport – a UK and London perspective. *International Journal of Sustainable Development, 12*(1), 24–47.

High-Level Panel on Water (HLPW). (2018). *Making Every Drop Count: An Agenda for Water Action*. https://bit.ly/3ZLU1T2.

Hofman-Bergholm, M. (2018). Could education for sustainable development benefit from a systems thinking approach? *Systems, 6*(4), 43–54.

Hofstede, G. (2011). Dimensionalizing cultures: the Hofstede model in context. *Online Readings in Psychology and Culture, 2*(1). https://doi.org/10.9707/2307-0919.1014.

Holdren, J. (2018). A brief history of IPAT. *Journal of Population and Sustainability, 2*(2), 66–74.

Hu, W. (2018, 18 January). A billion-dollar investment in New York's water. *New York Times*.

Hunt, C. F., Wilson, H. L., & Voulvoulis, N. (2020). Evaluating alternatives to plastic microbeads in cosmetics. *Nature Sustainability, 4*, 366–72.

Hynes, W., Lees, M., & Müller, J. (2020). *Systemic Thinking for Policy Making: The Potential of Systems Analysis for Addressing Global Policy Challenges in the 21st Century*. New Approaches to Economic Challenges series. Paris: OECD Publishing. https://doi.org/10.1787/879c4f7a-en.

IBM. (2012). *Leading Through Connections*. Global C-Suite Study series. www.intec.co.uk/wp-content/uploads/2014/08/IBM-CEO-study-2012.pdf.

IBM. (2022, 23 January). Yara and IBM launch an open collaboration for farm and field data to advance sustainable food production. https://bit.ly/3LFN5Ba.

Inauen, M., & Schenker-Wicki, A. (2012). Fostering radical innovations with open innovation. *European Journal of Innovation Management, 15*, 212–31.

Intergovernmental Panel on Climate Change (IPCC). (2020). *Global Warming of 1.5°C*. https://bit.ly/3Q1iEIb.

Intergovernmental Panel on Climate Change (IPCC). (2022). *Climate Change 2022: Impacts, Adaptation and Vulnerability*. www.ipcc.ch/report/ar6/wg2/.

Intergovernmental Panel on Climate Change (IPCC). (2023). *AR6 Synthesis Report*. www.ipcc.ch/report/sixth-assessment-report-cycle/.

International Commission on Financing Global Education Opportunity. (2016). *The Learning Generation: Investing in Education for a Changing World*. https://bit.ly/45mXqIV.

International Energy Agency (IEA). (2022). Data centres and data transmission networks. https://bit.ly/46pr9lE.

International Monetary Fund. (n.d.). Climate change | fossil fuel subsidies. www.imf.org/en/Topics/climate-change/energy-subsidies.

IPBES (Intergovernmental Science-Policy Platform on Biodiversity and Ecosystem Services). (2019). *Global Assessment Report on Biodiversity and Ecosystem Services*. www.ipbes.net/global-assessment.

Islam, M. S., & Kieu, E. (2020). Tackling regional climate change impacts and food security issues: a critical analysis across ASEAN, PIF, and SAARC. *Sustainability*, *12*(3), 883–903. https://doi.org/10.3390/su12030883.

Iversen, K. (2020, 17 December). Oat milk nation: how Covid changed how we drink. Before the pandemic, oat milk was on the rise – now it's everywhere. *Refinery29*. www.refinery29.com/en-gb/2020/12/10232640/oat-milk-rise-covid.

Jia, F., Zuluaga-Cardona, L., Bailey, A., & Rueda, X. (2018). Sustainable supply chain management in developing countries: an analysis of the literature. *Journal of Cleaner Production*, *189*, 263–78.

Johnstone, P., Stirling, A., & Sovacool, B. (2017). Policy mixes for incumbency: exploring the destructive recreation of renewable energy, shale gas 'fracking,' and nuclear power in the United Kingdom. *Energy Research & Social Science*, *33*, 147–62.

Kahneman, D. (2011). *Thinking, Fast and Slow*. New York: Farrar, Straus and Giroux.

Kapetaniou, C., & Rieple, A. (2017). The role of business ecosystems in the building of disruptive innovations. *Academy of Management*, *2017*(1). https://bit.ly/3EXqzjo.

Kapetaniou, C., Rieple, A., Pilkington, A., Frandsen, T., & Pisano, P. (2018). Building the layers of a new manufacturing taxonomy: how 3D printing is creating a new landscape of production eco-systems and competitive dynamics. *Technological Forecasting and Social Change*, *128*, 22–35.

Karp, T. (2006). Transforming organisations for organic growth: the DNA of change leadership. *Journal of Change Management*, *6*(1), 3–20.

Kates, R. W., Travis, W. R., & Wilbanks, T. J. (2012). Transformational adaptation when incremental adaptations to climate change are insufficient. *Proceedings of the National Academy of Sciences*, *109*(19), 7156–61.

KBV Research. (2022). *Global Everything as a Service (XaaS) Market Size, Share & Industry Trends Analysis Report by Organization Size, Vertical, Offering, Type, Regional Outlook and Forecast, 2022–2028.* https://bit.ly/46INcUE.

Keane, P. (2020, 20 September). How the oil industry made us doubt climate change. *BBC News.*

Kemp, R., Loorbach, D., & Rotmans, J. (2007). Transition management as a model for managing processes of co-evolution towards sustainable development. *International Journal of Sustainable Development & World Ecology, 14*(1), 78–91.

Kenny, M., & Meadowcroft, J. (eds.) (1999). *Planning Sustainability.* Abingdon, UK: Routledge.

Kim, R. E. (2023). Augment the SDG indicator framework. *Environmental Science and Policy, 142*(2023), 62–7.

Kingston, C., & Caballero, G. (2009). Comparing theories of institutional change. *Journal of Institutional Economics, 5*(2), 151–80.

Kohler, T. (2016). Corporate accelerators: building bridges between corporations and startups. *Business Horizons, 59*, 347–57.

Kramer, M. R., Kania, J., & Senge, P. (2018). *The Water of Systems Change.* Boston, MA: FSG. http://efc.issuelab.org/resources/30855/30855.pdf.

Kuznets, S. (1934). *National Income, 1929–1932.* 73rd US Congress, 2nd session, Senate document no. 124, p. 7. www.nber.org/system/files/chapters/c2258/c2258.pdf.

Laininen, E. (2018). Transforming our worldview towards a sustainable future. In J. W. Cook (ed.), *Sustainability, Human Well-Being, and the Future of Education*, 161–200. Cham: Palgrave Macmillan.

Lazaroiu, G., Andronie, M., Uță, C., & Hurloiu, I. (2019). Trust management in organic agriculture: sustainable consumption behavior, environmentally conscious purchase intention, and healthy food choices. *Frontiers in Public Health, 7*, 340.

Leach, M., Scoones, I., & Stirling, A. (2010). Governing epidemics in an age of complexity: narratives, politics and pathways to sustainability. *Global Environmental Change, 20*(3), 369–77.

Leijten, I. (2019). Human rights v. insufficient climate action: the Urgenda case. *Netherlands Quarterly of Human Rights, 37*(2), 112–18.

Levi, P. (2021, 23 March). *Iron and Steel Technology Roadmap.* (PowerPoint OECD Steel Committee). www.oecd.org/industry/ind/Item_10_IEA.pdf.

Loorbach, D. (2010). Transition management for sustainable development: a prescriptive, complexity-based governance framework. *Governance, 23*(1), 161–83.

Malerba, F. (2002). Sectoral systems of innovation and production. *Research Policy, 31*(2), 247–64.

Maon, F., Lindgreen, A., & Swaen, V. (2010). Organizational stages and cultural phases: a critical review and a consolidative model of CSR development. *International Journal of Management Reviews, 12*(1), 20–38.

Marsella, S., & Gratch, J. (2002). A step toward irrationality: using emotion to change belief. *Proceedings of the First International Joint Conference on Autonomous Agents and Multiagent Systems, 1*, 334–41.

Mazzucato, M. (2018). Mission-oriented innovation policies: challenges and opportunities. *Industrial and Corporate Change, 27*(5), 803–15.

McGann, M., Wells, T., & Blomkamp, E. (2021). Innovation labs and co-production in public problem solving. *Public Management Review, 23*(2), 297–316.

McKinsey & Company. (2022, 29 June). *Driven by Purpose: 15 Years of M-Pesa's Evolution.* https://bit.ly/48w4Pst.

McPhearson, T., Iwaniec, D. M., & Bai, X. (2016). Positive visions for guiding urban transformations toward sustainable futures. *Current Opinion in Environmental Sustainability, 22*, 33–40.

McPhearson, T., Raymond, C. M., Gulsrud, N., et al. (2021). Radical changes are needed for transformations to a good Anthropocene. *Urban Sustainability 1*(5). https://doi.org/10.1038/s42949-021-00017-x.

McVeigh, K., & Holliani Cahya, G. (2022, 1 August). Single servings at low prices: how Unilever's sachets became an environmental scourge. *Guardian.*

Meadows, D. (1999). *Leverage Points: Places to Intervene in a System.* Hartland, VT: Sustainability Institute. https://bit.ly/45fUKwE.

Meadows, D. H., Meadows, D. L., & Randers, J. (1992). *Beyond the Limits: Confronting Global Collapse, Envisioning a Sustainable Future.* White River Junction, VT: Chelsea Green.

Microsoft. (n.d.). *Climate Innovation Fund.* https://bit.ly/3F2hANI.

Midgley, G., & Lindhult, E. (2021). A systems perspective on systemic innovation. *Systems Research and Behavioral Science, 38*(5), 635–70.

Miller, M. L., & Vaccari, C. (2020). Digital threats to democracy: comparative lessons and possible remedies. *International Journal of Press/Politics, 25*(3), 333–56.

Milmo, D. (2023, 3 February). ChatGPT reaches 100 million users two months after launch. *Guardian.*

Mishra, J. L., Chiwenga, K. D., & Ali, K. (2019). Collaboration as an enabler for circular economy: a case study of a developing country. *Management Decision, 59*(8), 1784–1800.

Mohr, L. A., Webb, D. J., & Harris, K. E. (2005). Do consumers expect companies to be socially responsible? The impact of corporate social responsibility on buying behavior. *Journal of Consumer Affairs*, *35*(1), 45–72.

Mongsawad, P. (2012). The philosophy of the sufficiency economy: a contribution to the theory of development. *Asia-Pacific Development Journal*, *17*, 123–43.

Morgan, D. (2022, 8 August). Analysis: Democrats score big wins on climate, drugs with $430 billion U.S. Senate bill. *Reuters*. https://bit.ly/3EZz9xV.

Moschner, S., Fink, A., Kurpjuweit, S., Wagner, S. M., & Herstatt, C. (2019). Toward a better understanding of corporate accelerator models. *Business Horizons*, *62*(5), 637–47.

Moura-Leite, R. C., & Padgett, R. C. (2011). Historical background of corporate social responsibility. *Social Responsibility Journal*, *7*(4), 528–39.

Mowery, D. (2012). Defense-related R&D as a model for 'Grand Challenges' technology policies. *Research Policy*, *41*, 1703–15.

Nagler, E. (2021). *Standing Still*. RAC Foundation. https://bit.ly/48wuwJv.

Nandi, S., Sarkis, J., Hervani, A., & Helms, M. (2021). Do blockchain and circular economy practices improve post COVID-19 supply chains? A resource-based and resource dependence perspective. *Industrial Management & Data Systems*, *121*(2), 333–63.

Ndaruhutse, S., Jones, C., & Riggall, A. (2019). *Why Systems Thinking Is Important for the Education Sector*. Reading, UK: Education Development Trust. https://files.eric.ed.gov/fulltext/ED603263.pdf.

Net Zero Tracker. (2022). *Net Zero Stocktake 2022*. https://zerotracker.net/analysis/net-zero-stocktake-2022.

Norgaard, R. B. (1995). Beyond materialism: a coevolutionary reinterpretation of the environmental crisis. *Review of Social Economy*, *53*(4), 475–92.

Norgaard, R. B. (2006). *Development Betrayed: The End of Progress and a Coevolutionary Revisioning of the Future*. Abingdon, UK: Routledge.

Palmberg, I., Hofman-Bergholm, M., Jeronen, E., & Yli-Panula, E. (2017). Systems thinking for understanding sustainability? Nordic student teachers' views on the relationship between species. *Identification, Biodiversity and Sustainable Development*, *7*(3), 72.

Parmar, B., Freeman, R. E., Harrison, J. S., et al. (2010). Stakeholder theory: the state of the art. *Academy of Management Annals*, *4*(1), 403–45.

Parry, I. W. H., Black, S., & Vernon, N. (2021). *Still Not Getting Energy Prices Right: A Global and Country Update of Fossil Fuel Subsidies*. IMF Working Paper WP/21/236. International Monetary Fund. https://bit.ly/3RKEoJG.

PBL Netherlands Environmental Assessment Agency. (2015). *Impact of Car Sharing on Mobility and CO_2 Emissions*. https://bit.ly/45hfxAf.

Pelling, M., & Manuel-Navarrete, D. (2011). From resilience to transformation: the adaptive cycle in two Mexican urban centers. *Ecology and Society, 16*(2). https://doi.org/10.5751/ES-04038-160211.

Polanyi, K. (1944). *The Great Transformation: The Political And Economic Origins Of Our time*. New York: Farrar & Rinehart.

PwC. (n.d.). Scope 3 emissions: four major challenges. https://bit.ly/3PGXIVf.

PwC. (2015). *The Sharing Economy*. https://bit.ly/3ZEKgG2.

PwC. (2022a). *Asset and Wealth Management Revolution 2022: Exponential Expectations for ESG*. https://bit.ly/3RKEKQw.

PwC. (2022b). Empowered chief sustainability officers: the key to remaining credible and competitive. https://bit.ly/46fiRgj.

Raworth, K. (2017). *Doughnut Economics: Seven Ways to Think Like a 21st-Century Economist*. London: Random House.

Reike, D., Vermeulen, W., & Witjes, S. (2018). The circular economy: new or refurbished as CE 3.0? Exploring controversies in the conceptualization of the circular economy through a focus on history and resource value retention options. *Resources, Conservation and Recycling, 135*, 246–64.

Reimers, K., & Li, M. (2012). Government driven model of institutional change through adoption of new technology: a case study of the failed pharmaceutical bidding and procurement platforms in China. *Chinese Management Studies, 6*(1), 53–64.

Ritson, H. (2022, 29 November). *Putting Profit Before Welfare: A Closer Look at India's Digital Identification System*. Center for Human Rights & Global Justice. https://bit.ly/3LI7Njy.

Rogers, N. (2019). *Law, Fiction and Activism in a Time of Climate Change*. Abingdon, UK: Routledge.

Ropers, N. (2004). From resolution to transformation: the role of dialogue projects. In A. Austin, M. Fischer & N. Ropers (eds.), *Transforming Ethnopolitical Conflict: The Berghof Handbook*, 255–70. Cham: Springer.

Roth, N. (2022, 12 January). Saving CO2 with car sharing. *Bewusstgrün*.

Rowbotham, S., McKinnon, M., Leach, J., & Lamberts, R. (2019). Does citizen science have the capacity to transform population health science? *Critical Public Health, 29*(1), 118–28.

Sagan, C. (1994). *Pale Blue Dot: A Vision of the Human Future in Space*. New York: Random House.

S&P Global Ratings. (2022). *Weather Warning: Assessing Countries' Vulnerability to Economic Losses from Physical Climate Risks*. https://bit.ly/46A34Zc.

Schebesta, H., & Candel, J. J. L. (2020). Game-changing potential of the EU's Farm to Fork Strategy. *Nature Food, 1*, 586–8.

Scheyvens, R., Banks, G., & Hughes, E. (2016). The private sector and the SDGs: the need to move beyond 'business as usual'. *Sustainable Development, 24*(6), 371–82.

Schicks, J. (2013). The definition and causes of microfinance over-indebtedness: a customer protection point of view. *Oxford Development Studies, 41*(Sup1), S95–S116.

Schulz, K., & Siriwardane, R. (2015). Depoliticised and technocratic: normativity and the politics of transformative adaptation. Earth System Governance Working Paper no. 33. https://doi.org/10.13140/RG.2.1.3858.8645.

Scitovsky, T. (1954). Two concepts of external economies. *Journal of Political Economy, 62*, 143–51.

Scoones, I., Stirling, A., Abrol, D., et al. (2015). Transformations to sustainability. STEPS Working Paper no. 104. Brighton, UK: STEPS Centre. https://bit.ly/3rqzXcg. https://steps-centre.org/publication/transformations-to-sustainability-wp104/

Senge, P. M., Lichtenstein, B. B., Kaeufer, K., Bradbury, H., & Carroll, J. S. (2007). Collaborating for systemic change. *MIT Sloan Management Review, 48*(2), 44–53.

Serfontein, S., Basson, J. S., & Burden, J. (2009). Mapping a transformation from a traditional to an entrepreneurial organisation: a South African case – original research. *SA Journal of Human Resource Management, 7*, 1–14.

Shell. (n.d.). *Nature-Based Solutions*. https://bit.ly/3Q2ZhOZ.

Simon, H. A. (1957). *Models of Man, Social and Rational: Mathematical Essays on Rational Human Behavior in a Social Setting*. New York: John Wiley.

Singh Khadka, N. (2023). COP28: why has an oil boss been chosen to head climate summit? *BBC News*.

Skapinker, M., & Daneshkhu, S. (2016, 29 September). Can Unilever's Paul Polman change the way we do business? *Financial Times*.

Smith, A., & Stirling, A. (2005). Social-ecological resilience and sociotechnical transitions: critical issues for sustainability governance. STEPS Working Paper no. 8. Brighton, UK: STEPS Centre. https://bit.ly/46yxjzP.

Sonenshein, S. (2010). We're changing—or are we? Untangling the role of progressive, regressive, and stability narratives during strategic change implementation. *Academy of Management Journal, 53*, 477–512.

Speed, M. (2022, 18 October). 'Green hushing' on the rise as companies keep climate plans from scrutiny. *Financial Times*.

Stave, K. A. (2002). Using system dynamics to improve public participation in environmental decisions. *System Dynamics Review, 18*(2), 139–67.

Stefano, F. D., Bagdadli, S., & Camuffo, A. (2018). The HR role in corporate social responsibility and sustainability: a boundary-shifting literature review. *Human Resource Management, 57*, 549–66.

Steinbauer, J. (2020, 4 March). Which is the greenest burger in the land? *Sierra Club*. https://bit.ly/48Du2B9.

Sterman, J. D., & Sweeney, L. B. (2007). Understanding public complacency about climate change: adults' mental models of climate change violate conservation of matter. *Climatic Change, 80*, 213–38.

Stirling, A. (2014). From sustainability to transformation: dynamics and diversity in reflexive governance of vulnerability. In A. Hommels, J. Mesman & W. E. Bijker (eds.), *Vulnerability in Technological Cultures: New Directions in Research and Governance*, 305–32. Cambridge, MA: MIT Press.

Strathern, M. (1997). Improving ratings: audit in the British university system. *European Review, 5*(3), 305–21.

Surowiecki, J. (2004). *The Wisdom of Crowds: Why the Many Are Smarter Than the Few*. New York: Anchor.

Swain, R. B. (2012). *The Microfinance Impact*. Abingdon, UK: Routledge.

Swinnen, J., & Kuijpers, R. (2019). Value chain innovations for technology transfer in developing and emerging economies: conceptual issues, typology, and policy implications. *Food Policy, 83*, 298–309.

Swiss Re. (2021). *The Economics of Climate Change: Climate Change Poses the Biggest Long-Term Risk to the Global Economy. No Action Is Not an Option*. https://bit.ly/46A4KSu.

Tan, E. K. (2020). From Third World to First World: law and policy in Singapore's urban transformation & integration. *Vietnamese Journal of Legal Sciences, 2*(1), 96–114.

Tang, A. (2019, 12 March). Inside Taiwan's new digital democracy. *Economist*.

Tanwar, A. S., Chaudhry, H., & Srivastava, M. K. (2022). Trends in influencer marketing: a review and bibliometric analysis. *Journal of Interactive Advertising, 22*(1), 1–27.

Temple-West, P., & Masters, B. (2023, 1 March). Wall Street titans confront ESG backlash as new financial risk. *Financial Times*.

The World Counts. (2023). *World Population Data Overview*. www.theworld counts.com/.

Thurman, B. (2014). *Oslo 2014, address Leadership Forum*. The Performance Theatre.

Tricks, H. (2022, 23 July). A broken idea: ESG investing. *Economist*.

Trucost. (2013). *Natural Capital at Risk: The Top 100 Externalities of Business*. https://bit.ly/46gFelG.

Tyler, S., & Moench, M. (2012). A framework for urban climate resilience. *Climate and Development, 4*(4), 311–26.

Unilever. (2020, May 12). Lessons learnt: business must drive systems change. https://bit.ly/48zgUx1.

Unilever Foundry. (n.d.). Level 3. *Co-working With Purpose.* https://l3.work/startupcommunity.

United Nations. (2022a). *2022 NDC Synthesis Report.* https://unfccc.int/ndc-synthesis-report-2022.

United Nations. (2022b). *The Sustainable Development Goals Report 2022.* https://unstats.un.org/sdgs/report/2022/.

United Nations Climate Change. (n.d.). *Race To Zero Campaign.* https://unfccc.int/climate-action/race-to-zero-campaign.

United Nations Environment Programme. (2021). *Adaptation Gap Report 2020.* https://bit.ly/3rCZVJC.

United Nations Framework Convention on Climate Change. (2016). *The Paris Agreement.* Bonn, Germany. https://unfccc.int/process-and-meetings/the-paris-agreement.

United Nations Principles of Responsible Investment. (2022). *Annual Report 2022.* www.unpri.org/annual-report-2022.

Vaara, E., Sonenshein, S., & Boje, D. M. (2016). Narratives as sources of stability and change in organizations: approaches and directions for future research. *Academy of Management Annals, 10,* 495–560.

Vakkuri, J., & Johanson, J. E. (2021). *Hybrid Governance, Organisations and Society: Value Creation Perspectives.* Abingdon, UK: Routledge.

Vakola, M., Soderquist, K. E., & Prastacos, G. P. (2007). Competency management in support of organisational change. *International Journal of Manpower, 28,* 260–75.

Valerdi, R., & Rouse, W. B. (2010). When systems thinking is not a natural act. *IEEE International Systems Conference,* 184–9.

Van der Zanden, G. J. (2022a). Leapfrogging from corporate social responsibility (CSR) to sustainability leadership. *Thai-American Business.*

Van der Zanden, G. J. (2022b, 4 October). Why the world needs systemic change. *AACSB.* https://bit.ly/3rFiAob.

Van der Zanden, G. J. (2023). Mindful leaders create positive societal impact. *AACSB.*

Vangen, S., Hayes, J. P., & Cornforth, C. (2015). Governing cross-sector, inter-organizational collaborations. *Public Management Review, 17*(9), 1237–60.

Vives, M.-L., & FeldmanHall, O. (2018). Tolerance to ambiguous uncertainty predicts prosocial behavior. *Nature Communications, 9*(2156). https://doi.org/10.1038/s41467-018-04631-9.

Vogt, M. (2021). Enlightenment 2.0: toward responsible science in the Anthropocene. In P. A. Wilderer, M. Grambow, M. Molls & K. Oexle (eds.), *Strategies for Sustainability of the Earth System*, 395–409. Cham: Springer.

Voulvoulis, N., Giakoumis, T., Hunt, C., et al. (2022). Systems thinking as a paradigm shift for sustainability transformation. *Global Environmental Change*, *75*(1), 102544.

Wagner, C., & Winkler, A. (2013). The vulnerability of microfinance to financial turmoil: evidence from the global financial crisis. *World Development*, *51*, 71–90.

Wang, J. (2016). Revive China's green GDP programme. *Nature*, *534*, 37.

Wardle, C., & Derakhshan, H. (2017). *Information Disorder: Toward an Interdisciplinary Framework for Research and Policy Making*. Council of Europe Report DGI(2017)09. https://bit.ly/3tgLHOS.

Waste2Wear. (n.d.). *What We Do*. www.waste2wear.com/about-us/what-we-do/.

Weenk, E., & Henzen, R. (2021). *Mastering the Circular Economy: A Practical Approach to the Circular Business Model Transformation*. London: Kogan Page.

Weick, K. E. (1984). Small wins: redefining the scale of social problems. *American Psychologist*, *39*(1), 40–9.

Wesseler, J. H. (2022). The EU's farm-to-fork strategy: An assessment from the perspective of agricultural economics. *Applied Economic Perspectives and Policy*, *44*(3), 1–18.

Wessner, C. (2003). Sustaining Moore's law and the US economy. *Computing in Science & Engineering*, *5*(1), 30–8.

Westley, F., Olsson, P., Folke, C., et al. (2011). Tipping toward sustainability: emerging pathways of transformation. *Ambio*, *40*, 762–80.

Wong, K. (2001, 9 April). Mother Nature's medicine cabinet. *Scientific American*.

Wood, W. (2000). Attitude change: persuasion and social influence. *Annual Review of Psychology*, *51*, 539–70.

World Bank. (2012, 17 May). *India: Issues and Priorities for Agriculture*. https://bit.ly/48E6gFm.

World Bank (Clement, V., Rigaud, K. K., de Sherbinin, A., et al.). (2021). *Groundswell Part 2: Acting on Internal Climate Migration*. Washington, DC: World Bank. http://hdl.handle.net/10986/36248.

World Bank. (2022). *Poverty and Shared Prosperity 2022*. https://bit.ly/45nvHYY.

World Bank. (2023). *GDP per capita, PPP (current international $)*. https://bit.ly/46pY9KU.

World Economic Forum (WEF), Ellen MacArthur Foundation & McKinsey & Company. (2016). *The New Plastics Economy – Rethinking the Future of Plastics*. https://bit.ly/45dGfcT.

World Economic Forum (WEF). (2020). *Nature Risk Rising: Why the Crisis Engulfing Nature Matters for Business and the Economy.* https://bit.ly/3ZEPm58.

World Economic Forum (WEF). (2023). *Global Risks Report 2023.* www.weforum.org/reports/global-risks-report-2023/.

World Inequality Lab. (2022). *World Inequality Report 2022.* https://wir2022.wid.world/.

Xynteo, GLTE & Royal Dutch Shell. (2016). *Collaboration for New Growth: Learning from Leaders.* https://issuu.com/xynteo/docs/collaboration_for_new_growth.

Yankelovich, D. (1999). *The Magic of Dialogue: Transforming Conflict into Cooperation.* New York: Touchstone.

Žalėnienė, I., & Pereira, P. (2021). Higher education for sustainability: a global perspective. *Geography and Sustainability, 2*(2), 99–106.

Acknowledgements

We want to thank the colleagues and critical minds that contributed valuable thoughts during the production of this Element. These include Charmaine Che, Warintorn Chokbancha, Ranjit Gupta, Dean Outerson, Alfonso Pellegrino, Niklas Rydberg, Pattarake Sarajoti, Piyawan Srioanchan, Iman Stratenus, Lars Svensson, Pinnaree Tea-makorn, Supakanda Tongboonrawd, Richard Welford, Steven White, Steven Young and, last but not least, Rosalind Yunibandhu.

Cambridge Elements ⹀

Reinventing Capitalism

Arie Y. Lewin

Duke University

Arie Y. Lewin is Professor Emeritus of Strategy and International Business at Duke University, Fuqua School of Business. He is an Elected Fellow of the Academy of International Business and a Recipient of the Academy of Management inaugural Joanne Martin Trailblazer Award. Previously, he was Editor-in-Chief of *Management and Organization Review* (2015–2021) and the *Journal of International Business Studies* (2000–2007), founding Editor-in-Chief of *Organization Science* (1989–2007), and Convener of Organization Science Winter Conference (1990–2012). His research centers on studies of organizations' adaptation as co-evolutionary systems, the emergence of new organizational forms, and adaptive capabilities of innovating and imitating organizations. His current research focuses on deglobalization and decoupling, the Fourth Industrial Revolution, and the renewal of capitalism.

Till Talaulicar

University of Erfurt

Till Talaulicar holds the Chair of Organization and Management at the University of Erfurt where he is also Dean of the Faculty of Economics, Law and Social Sciences. His main research expertise is in the areas of corporate governance and the responsibilities of the corporate sector in modern societies. Professor Talaulicar is Editor-in-Chief of *Corporate Governance: An International Review*, Senior Editor of *Management and Organization Review* and serves on the Editorial Board of *Organization Science*. Moreover, he has been Founding Member and Chairperson of the Board of the International Corporate Governance Society (2014–2020).

About the Series

This series seeks to feature explorations about the crisis of legitimacy facing capitalism today, including the increasing income and wealth gap, the decline of the middle class, threats to employment due to globalization and digitalization, undermined trust in institutions, discrimination against minorities, global poverty and pollution. Being grounded in a business and management perspective, the series incorporates contributions from multiple disciplines on the causes of the current crisis and potential solutions to renew capitalism.

Panmure House is the final and only remaining home of Adam Smith, Scottish philosopher and 'Father of modern economics.' Smith occupied the House between 1778 and 1790, during which time he completed the final editions of his master works: *The Theory of Moral Sentiments* and *The Wealth of Nations*. Other great luminaries and thinkers of the Scottish Enlightenment visited Smith regularly at the House across this period. Their mission is to provide a world-class 21st-century centre for social and economic debate and research, convening in the name of Adam Smith to effect positive change and forge global, future-focussed networks.

ADAM SMITH
PANMURE
HOUSE

Cambridge Elements ≡

Reinventing Capitalism

Elements in the Series

A full series listing is available at: www.cambridge.org/RECA

Printed in the United States
by Baker & Taylor Publisher Services